A Beautiful Country

A Beautiful Language

Exploring Italy
and its Language

Jack Dewhurst

SUMMERSDALE

Summersdale Publishers
46 West Street
Chichester
West Sussex
PO19 1RP
England

A CIP catalogue for this book is available from the British Library.

Printed and bound in Great Britain
by Biddles Ltd., Guildford and Kings Lynn

ISBN 1 873475 17 9

*To our good friends Geoffrey and Mary
whose suggestion started it all.*

Contents

Chapter 1
La Dogana
The Custom House...................................7

Chapter 2
Il Palazzo Galengo...............................24

Chapter 3
La Campagna
The Countryside.................................36

Chapter 4
Ancora La Scuola
Back to School................................51

Chapter 5
Perugia..63

Chapter 6
Cesenatico..81

Chapter 7
Urbania...101

Chapter 1

La Dogana
The Custom House

We have been carrying on a love affair for years. I don't just mean with each other - although that too since we are husband and wife - but with Italy.

Hazel believes that it was love at first sight and she may be right. Certainly the first time we ever visited that wonderful country we were captivated by its people, its countryside, its medieval towns and villages, its culture, its food and wine but, above all, by its language. It is difficult to understand why a language, of which, at that time, we could not speak a word, should have had such an attraction for us. But, there it was; this beautiful language - *questa bella lingua* - was something we simply had to learn.

We began to read elementary books of the 'Teach yourself Italian' type. We went to a few night classes which were not a success since our brains switch off around seven o' clock in the evening. We had intermittent private lessons from young Italians, living in England, who wished to earn a little extra money. And of course we went to Italy whenever we could which was seldom more that once a year. Each time we returned from a visit there we felt we had made progress but, by the time we went again, we realised how much we had forgotten.

After my retirement we were able to go to Adult Education Classes during the daytime and also to have private lessons from the teacher, a charming Italian lady who had lived in England for many years. We got a little better, it is true, but we wanted not only to get better but to get better quicker before we became too old to learn anything. But the problem was how?

It was an Australian friend who provided a possible solution. 'What you two ought to do,' he said one day, quite casually, 'is to go to the University for Foreigners in Perugia. Lots of Australians go there. I'm sure you would enjoy it since you love the language so much.'

This was the first we had heard of a University in Italy which taught Italian to foreigners. It was certainly an attractive notion but would it be foolish to go at our age? Would a septuagenarian and his wife even be accepted? Although, in some ways, it appeared to be a foolhardy venture, the more we thought about it the more appealing it became.

'We could always write off and get the prospectus,' said Hazel, who was clearly warming to the idea. 'There's no harm in that. We could have a look at it and then make up our minds.'

Writing to the University of Perugia for a prospectus was a task for which our Italian tuition, up to that time, had not prepared us. Our instruction had been concerned almost entirely with simple conversational Italian -

'Good morning, how are you?'

'Can I have the bill please?'

'Do you take credit cards?' -

that sort of thing. We had scarcely written a letter of any kind and certainly not to an important official of a university.

How was the Director to be addressed? We had learned enough to know that we could not just translate 'Dear Sir' into Italian - *Caro Signore*. We felt that something more elaborate and formal was called for. We consulted our dictionary which offered us several possibilities. There was *Egregio Direttore* - 'Notable Director'; or *Illustre Direttore* - 'Illustrious Director'; or even *Illustrissimo Direttore* - 'Most Illustrious Director'. Wishing to impress we chose the latter and, with some difficulty and repeated consultations of the dictionary, we made our request for a copy of the University's prospectus, adding the fact that we were senior citizens, in case that mattered.

Eventually the document arrived by which time we were becoming so enthusiastic that we would probably have decided to go whatever information it contained. In fact it all seemed most favourable and not expensive. We could go, it seemed, for one, two, three, six or twelve months for around £110.00 a month. The University might be able to help us to find suitable accommodation but this would be either with a family, which did not appeal, or in a hotel which appealed even less. We wanted an apartment and, if we were going to find one we would have to do it ourselves. Nothing was said about our advanced age.

So far so good we thought, and we signed on for a four weeks course in January when nothing would need doing in our garden.

Filled with zeal for further learning we set about trying to find an apartment when we met our first snag. The various rental and travel agencies we approached in London were either dismissive that anyone should want a flat in Perugia in January or ignorant about where Perugia actually was. We asked help from an Italian friend in London who passed on the request to her friend in Italy, but time went by and no success was reported. We became anxious then desperate that we might have to live in a tent. Then, a short time before we were due to leave, a message came through. A flat had been found, not in Perugia itself but in a village called Tuoro, some twenty kilometres outside the city, by the shores of Lake Trasimeno. The apartment was in a building called *La Dogana*, the Custom House.

We had thought of renting a car for the duration of our course, and this was now essential if we were to drive into the city of Perugia every day. Our travel agent gave us the choice of flying to Bologna or Pisa and renting a car there. Both seemed a long way from Umbria and there seemed nothing to choose between them in terms of distance. We chose Bologna, a happy choice, as it turned out, since it was a small airport with none of the hassle of a larger one. Our Fiat Uno was awaiting us and off we went without delay down the A.1. Autostrada which runs from Milan to Rome.

It was a delightful drive although a long one. Since we were, for the most part, travelling during the lunch hour and its following siesta time, there were relatively few cars on the road and we had an easy task adjusting to a left hand drive car on the right hand side of the road. Once we found our way out of Bologna much of the road was mountainous and we passed through many tunnels - *Gallerie*, and quite spectacular at times. At a large junction south of Arrezzo we turned off onto a *raccordo* - a connecting road - which carried traffic from the west to the east of the country, and within a short time we were at Tuoro.

We turned off the raccordo into a narrow street decorated with Christmas lights since we were still more than a week away from twelfth night. At a garage towards the end of the street we asked a man for directions. We were to turn left and go for perhaps 2 kilometres; we would see La Dogana easily since it had many arches -

'molte arche' - along the front of it. And he added, we think, 'you can't miss it'.

Which was why we were standing before a massive building in Umbria, on a Saturday afternoon, in winter, preparing to be University students again, in two days time, after a lapse of a great many years.

So, this gigantic stone edifice was La Dogana. It was enormous and forbidding. There were, indeed, seven or eight large arches along its frontage with the road leading into a portico which extended along the whole length of the building. Our surprise that we should be living in such a place turned to astonishment when we approached the front door and read a notice on the wall beside it.

The notice read: -

Under this portico on the border between the Granduchy and the Papal States, innumerable travellers stopped for inspection and a change of horses; from Michelangelo to Galileo, from Goethe to Lord Byron and Stendhal.

There was more but we were unable to translate it. Hazel at last broke the silence.

'Well,' she said, 'we certainly are in good company.'

And so we were and the effect on us was startling. We had no idea what sort of place we might have been coming to but, as we stood there in silence, in company it seemed with majestic, historical figures such as these we felt that already we had left the 20th century behind and were back in medieval Italy. It was a feeling which would quickly be reinforced.

We pushed open a large door and entered a bleak stone flagged hallway. There was barely enough light to see our way up a long flight of stone steps. As we made our ascent I thought I could just make out a figure standing in wait for us at the top. Perhaps he would be able to take us where we were supposed to go? But there was no word of welcome; why was he so silent? A few steps more and I realised that we would get no information out of him. He was a wooden statue of a monk, life sized and wearing a brown habit. His hand was outstretched as if in greeting but, as I got nearer I could see that it had once held a lantern although, now, there was only the hole from which this had been removed, who can say how many years before.

I turned my head to see that Hazel was watching him spellbound, I groped around on the wall to try to find a light which revealed, behind the monk, a startling wall painting which would have made Michelangelo feel very much at home. Medieval knights and their ladies, their paint peeling off the wall in many places, peered over the battlements of a large castle which showed similar ravages.

Once more we gazed in silence at this surprising apparition when my wife spoke again.

'Come on. There seem to be about four more flights. Let's go up and try to find someone to help us.'

We had barely mounted two steps, however, when a door slammed above us and a slight, dark Italian bounded down the stairs towards us, pulling on a jacket as he came. I was still summoning up some kind of greeting in Italian when he burst into English.

'Professor and Mrs Dewhurst?'

The letter 'H' defeats all but the most fluent Italians, and 'Dewhurst' emerged more like 'Duust'.

He held out his hand and was full of apologies. His name was Emanuele. He was glad to see us. We were earlier than he had expected and he had been enjoying a rest after his lunch. But all was well now. We were here and he would show us up to our apartment. Only three more flights.

We trudged up the stairs after him. He talked happily as we got higher and higher. Our apartment was at the top of the stairs on the right, he said, his was on the left where he lived with his wife, Paola, and his young son. Paola had no English but the boy was learning and would be glad to talk to us. But here was the flat. Please to come in and he would show us everything.

Despite the antiquity of the building with its monkish statues and wall paintings we were totally unprepared for what 'everything' might include. We walked into an enormous lounge with a long refectory-type table and chairs at the far end near the windows, and an L shaped arrangement of long settees by a low coffee table in the middle of the room. In the centre of the wall behind these settees was a massive iron range - which we soon learned with relief we were not expected to use - whilst the opposite wall was entirely covered by a tapestry some twenty five feet in length, depicting a medieval hunting scene, with various swains and damsels desporting themselves in the background.

The three bedrooms each contained a double bed with another single bed in two of them. With eight people in the beds and four more on the the huge settees, twelve people could have been comfortably accommodated in the flat without any difficulty. Since we were only two we began making mental lists of all the friends we might ask to stay. There was a long utilitarian kitchen, well stocked with pots and pans, knives and forks, cooking implements of all kinds and some four dozen assorted tumblers and wine glasses. But just as the apartment was designed for a large number of people so was the kitchen equipment. One could have made spaghetti for twelve in any of the large containers but to find a pan small enough to boil an egg was impossible. We later borrowed one from Paola.

It was the shower - *la doccia* - which caused us the greatest anxiety. True to the medieval ambience of the place it was medieval in its appearance and function. 'Shower' suggests a fine spray of water, preferably hot; our *doccia* produced a single steady stream which, if we were lucky, might, from time to time, bifurcate into two steady streams which were sometimes warm but seldom hot.

But we were prepared to take the rough with the smooth - or as an Italian would say *il buono e le cattive*, the good and the bad, and, by and large, the faded elegance of our apartment, redolent of habitation by distinguished personages of times past, constituted the smooth.

Once we had unpacked Emanuele invited us into his flat to meet his wife and child. They were an interesting family. Emanuele's father had been a diplomat and there had, therefore, been a lot of travelling about in his youth. This was probably one reason why his English was so good although he was anxious that it should be better; for this reason we always talked to him in English although we would have preferred to do so in Italian. He was following a course in hotel management and was doing the job of caretaker of La Dogana as a temporary measure.

He explained about La Dogana, the Custom House. Several hundred years earlier Perugia, and its surrounding region, had been a Papal State owing its temporal allegiance to the Popes. Thus, those entering or leaving had to pass through the customs, even such distinguished personages as Michelangelo, Galileo, Lord Byron, Goethe and

Stendhal. We later learned that there had been frequent Perugian revolts against this rule which had been put down by Papal troops with varying degrees of ferocity. It was not until 1860, during the revolution which led ultimately to the unification of Italy - *il Resorgimento* - that the Papal yoke was finally thrown off.

Emanuele and Paola were extremely kind to us during our stay, and went out of their way to make us comfortable. He kept a close eye on everything, making sure the central heating was working well, for example, and if the weather was mild and we were out in the afternoon, as we usually were, he would come in and turn off a few radiators so that our heating bill would not be too large. Paola, of course, knew all the best shops and told us where to find them.

We asked if we could go to Mass that Saturday evening. Yes, they said, at 5 o' clock and by that time the shops would be open and we could buy whatever we needed. If we went to the shops Paola mentioned, and told them who we were and where we were staying, we could be sure of good service.

Off we went into the town to find the Parish Church which was on a little hill with convenient parking spaces nearby. It was a surprisingly large church, with several statues of saints, who are a special interest of mine. I was pleased to see St Rocco, a favourite in Italy, although seldom seen in England. He was a professional pilgrim during the 11th century and, on his journeys, he encountered the plague several times and helped to nurse its victims. Eventually he too contracted the disease and, to avoid spreading it among the others in the town, he went off into the woods where, legend says, a dog brought him a loaf of bread every day in its mouth. In art he is shown pointing to a plague spot on his leg and there is often a dog at his feet. He is the patron saint of plague sufferers and, of course, of dogs!

We introduced ourselves to the Parish Priest who was pleased to have some English visitors but who had to rush off to say Mass somewhere else. We went off on our shopping expedition to make contact with the locals. Tuoro - or to give it its full name Tuoro sul Trasimeno - was merely a village but with a surprising number of elegant shops. We were each to buy a thick, warm jersey there before our stay was out. We chose a small *alimentare* in the main square for our purchases and were warmly welcomed as Paola said we would be.

Eventually, well supplied with everything we required, we returned to La Dogana, saluted the monk on the way upstairs and settled down for a quiet evening after a tiring but successful day. Hazel was determined to give the medieval kitchen a try out if only for something simple, such as omelettes, followed by fruit and cheese; anything more adventurous would have to wait until another night.

With somewhere comfortable to live - and it could not be denied that our apartment had, at least, the outward appearance of luxury - we needed to get down to work which, of course, meant preparing to attend the Italian University for Foreigners - 'L'Università Italiana per Stranieri'. We would have no problem in getting to Perugia itself. We had our rental car and Emanuele had told us that there was a fast dual carriageway all the way into the city. But, with the maze of narrow Italian streets to contend with, would we find it easy to reach the university? Here again Emanuele was a great help - or so we thought at the time.

He produced a modern map and showed us the university area which was at the apex of the city. From a wide base Perugia goes steadily up and up until, leaving the more modern areas behind, the old historic centre - *il centro storico -* is reached. Emanuele's map, with its throughways, flyovers and underpasses, showed how misleading was an old one we had borrowed in England from a colleague who had once been to Perugia years before. Emanuele was eloquent in describing what we had to do. We were to come off the dual carriageway at the next exit after the one marked *Ferro di Cavallo* - horse shoe. Then we would go left, then right towards the railway station, up this hill, round that corner... and so it went on. Sadly we realised that, even were we able to follow these instructions to the letter, we would still not have reached the *centro storico* with its labyrinth of narrow passages which led to the university buildings.

We had one thing in our favour, however. We had had the foresight to arrive on Saturday and so, if necessary, we would have the whole of Sunday to find our way around when, hopefully, there would be less traffic on the roads. We needed most of it.

Our first contact with the city proper found us on the right road but going in the wrong direction. When our surroundings became more and more industrial we were obliged to stop and ask for directions. Greatly uplifted by having held a successful conversation with an Italian, we retraced our steps.

Soon the railway station appeared before us. We knew Emanuele had mentioned this, but which of the three roads leading away from it were we to take? There was one to the right, one to the left and a third which plunged below the railway lines. Was this the one he had mentioned? We thought it was. So far, so good, but two circuits of the town found us back at the station again each time although we were, at least, on the right side of the tracks. We pulled into a side road and stopped. Out came the map. Where were we? After some disagreement we decided that if we were here we should have gone up this road instead of that one. Very well, let's try it.

We did with no better luck. We seemed to have been driving around for hours.

Desperation was fast becoming despair and we might well have gone home, except that we did not know the way. Then - and we will never know how - it all slotted into place. From a large road junction with traffic lights, which we were fairly certain we had seen at least twice before, we took a right turn up a narrow one way street, past two car parks, virtually empty on that Sunday morning, turned right through a long tunnel - The Galleria Kennedy - down a hill and up the other side, transversed, with great trepidation, a narrow archway and emerged into the Piazza Fortebraccio - 'strongarm' - named after a famous fighter of long ago.

And there before us, in all its glory, was the seat of learning for all foreigners wishing to become fluent in Italian or even just to rub along in the bars and restaurants and in casual conversation with the locals - *Il Palazzo Galengo*.

We pulled over to the side of the piazza for a moment and surveyed it. The palazzo was a massive stone, square building, hermetically sealed that Sunday morning. To our left, as we looked at it, was an enormous Etruscan Gate through which, we later learned, a narrow hill led upwards to the Duomo and the main part of the city centre. Opposite the pallazo was a tiny park, and down beside this was a narrow road which would lead us, Emanuele had said, to a car park.

We took it all in, scarcely able to believe that we had actually found it, then we headed home to Tuoro for a late lunch, delighted that we had battled successfully to achieve our goal - and, that afternoon, we went back and did it all again just to be sure.

Back, finally, at La Dogana in the early evening, we began to assemble the few things we had brought from England which we thought we would be likely to need - various dictionaries, one large for our homework - *il compito* - and two small to carry around with us. We had notebooks, pens, pencils and two rubbers for the many mistakes we felt sure we would make.

There were also other items we had had the foresight to bring with us from England - gin, tonic and a lemon, to mention three. Now was the time to sit back and celebrate our victory over the Perugian traffic system. Sitting in the faded splendour of a bygone age, with modern restoratives to hand, was beginning to grow on us. A month here would suit us quite nicely. Our kitchen and the multitude of items it contained would surely lend itself to Hazel's well known culinary skill. But not tonight; tonight we needed a local restaurant with some good Italian home cooking to round off the day. Emanuele had mentioned one not far away and we set off to sample the fare. What was served was excellent -

crostini, tagliatelle alla salsa d'uova and a *tiramisu.* The only decision we had to make about the wine was whether we wanted red or white!

That night we slept like babies, folded in a blanket of times past and present and well prepared, we hoped, for whatever tomorrow might bring.

Chapter 2

Il Palazzo Galengo

The process of registration for our course of instruction in the Italian language at the university for foreigners in Perugia is inadequately described as *L'iscrizione*.

We were up and about early that first Monday morning and we entered the portals of the Palazzo Galengo well before 8.00 am. The reception area was empty but, down a narrow corridor and continuing on down some steps towards the basement, a crowd of young people of all shapes, sizes and colours had gathered. Were we to join them? Was the registration in the basement? Whom could we ask? Did any of the notices on the walls of the corridor tell us what to do? They did not, so, dismayed by the increasing number of students thronging the corridor, we fled to the Bar Roma across the piazza.

The Bar Roma produced high quality cappuccino both on that morning and throughout our stay. It was usually crowded with students, some from our class and some from others and it provided the refreshment and the relaxation we so much needed after the concentration we had to give to our lessons each day.

Two cappuccinos behind us we attempted once more to reach the room, where, we hoped, we would be registered. The mass of students in the corridor had, mercifully, reduced significantly, and eventually we found ourselves in the basement, before a window in a long counter which, we were told, was where we should begin.

'Your two photographs, please,' said the lady behind the window, adding, 'no?' when she saw the blank looks on our faces.

'You must have two photographs each,' she explained, 'and a photocopy of each of your passports.'

She directed us back outside the building and around a corner to a photographer's shop from which, within a very short time, we emerged with criminal-type photographs and photocopies of our passports.

'10,000 Lire, please,' the man said, and we paid him willingly.

Approaching the same counter lady once more we completed whatever requirements she had, and we were directed to another window.

There our photographs were fixed onto cards which, we were told, we must carry at all times, and then this lady said,

'Now your stamps please.'

More blank looks from us resulted in our being instructed to obtain two stamps (10,000 Lire each) to make our registration legal. Back outside once more, we dodged across the speeding traffic in the piazza to the postcard shop - *la cartelleria* - on the opposite corner to spend another 20,000 Lire. Once these expensive stamps had been applied to the forms relating to each of us, we were sent across to the opposite wall where two ladies sat at a desk.

Would we please do a small test, we were asked, to see into which class we should be put. It would be an exaggeration to say that this test was, in any sense, difficult, but our state of mind was scarcely conducive to serious mental activity. Somehow we completed the test, and within two minutes it was corrected and we were assigned to level two - *livello due*. We had reason to be grateful for that.

There was one last hurdle to be surmounted but we did not succeed in doing it then nor for several days afterwards. We needed to register with the police - *la polizia*.

There had evidently been a time when such registration was either not required or was not enforced, but with foreign students coming into Italy from all over the world, the University provided one possible means of illegal entry or, at any rate, of unregistered entry. Such *clandestini*, as they were called, had managed to get in for years by one means or another and many were exploited in manual work of all kinds for little reward, or else they drifted into drugs or crime or both. The registration system, with which we were about to contend, was clearly essential.

It was far from easy to accomplish, nonetheless.

The ladies who had assigned us to *livello due* could see through an adjoining window that the queue for this formality was huge. 'Queue' was in any event too strong a word. A mass of students, four of five deep in places, thronged a narrow corridor and, as we later discovered when we eventually reached this point, jockeyed for position through an even narrower doorway to stand, finally, before two policemen who were checking what was already written on duplicated forms, and asking more questions.

'What was our address in Perugia?' It was not in Perugia but outside it.

'Nevertheless, what was it?' The address of La Dogana was provided.

'Were we on the telephone?' Emanuele was but we were not and it seemed easier to say no.

'Had we a motor car?' Yes, we had.

'What was its number?' Hazel, fortunately, had made a note of this in her diary.

'Did we own the car or was it rented?' It was a rental car.

And so on.

Not for three days were we able to find the number of jostling students small enough to attempt to join them and, eventually, to achieve registration. Had it not been for the kind lady - *la Signora molto gentile* - who assigned us to *livello due* we might have missed the entire first morning's instruction completely. As it was she took pity on us and gave us a temporary card which we could use until we were able to complete the policeman's requirements.

Armed with temporary registration, at least, we were instructed to go to *aula cinque*. *Aula* was not a word we had previously encountered although we would come across it many times, over the years, in different schools in Italy. Our bewilderment must have been clearly evident in our blank faces.

'Classroom five,' she translated. 'First floor.'

The hassle of registration had not allowed us any real opportunity to take stock of our surroundings. Emerging from the basement like two divers coming up for air, we were once again in the entrance hall which was spacious, stone flagged but somewhat forbidding. The information room, which was now going strong answering the questions of students who were, no doubt, as perplexed as we had been, occupied one wall. On the opposite side was a bank so we would have no need to rush off into the city to change money; with the number of 10,000 Lire notes we were disbursing an early visit there seemed to be highly likely. A wide flight of stone steps led upwards, we imagined, to *aula cinque*.

After checking to make sure that we had no immediate need to go into the bank, we made our way up the stairs, puffing with exertion as we did so. Several youthful students passed us at the double - oh to be young again. We finally reached the top where a notice directed us to classrooms one to five and we followed the signs gratefully. *Aula cinque* was down a few steps at the end of a short corridor. The door was open and the sounds of chattering students could be heard from within.

We had evidently missed nothing, our student colleagues, we assumed, having been delayed by the interminable registration process almost as long as we had. There were perhaps some forty to fifty students dotted around at various points on long benches which rose steeply to large windows at the back. A hundred students could easily have been accommodated there and, despite the number present, there were still plenty of empty seats. We slipped into two on the front row and waited for something to happen. We became directly involved sooner than we expected.

The professor, who was arranging papers at a small desk in front of the class, put them on one side and came out towards us to start the proceedings.

To say that we were filled with anxiety was to understate the case. We had come back to be university students again, at a foreign university, where all the teaching would, inevitably, be in Italian, some forty years after our own university careers had come to an end. Was this a foolhardy enterprise? Would we be able to keep up with the bright young people behind us? A couple of backward glances around the class had suggested that we were at least thirty years older than the next most senior person in the room. I could not help recalling the words of one of my colleagues in London when I told him what we intended to do.

'What an intellectual challenge,' he had remarked.

Challenge it undoubtedly was, but would our intellects be up to it?

The professor, to whom we were thereafter ever grateful, immediately put our minds at rest. He began to speak in clear, precise Italian, never bursting into torrents of rapid utterance as did many Italians we would meet. He told us who he was - Professor Silvestrini - and he was pleased to see us all. He and several of his colleagues would be our teachers for the next month. We would be following a text book which he, and two other professors had recently published, and we were encouraged to buy it (30,000 Lire this time) so as to be able to keep up easily with each lesson. Now he would like us to tell him who we were and where we came from.

And he pointed at me!

The fact of our advanced age must, already, have been apparent to all, and it must have seemed probable that, sitting together as we were in the front row, we were either married or cohabiting (living in sin, which was a common phrase in our youth, no longer having any significance). Nevertheless, when it became Hazel's turn to speak, after I had given my short spiel, and she announced that we were man and wife, we got a great cheer which got everyone into a happy mood.

As the various students introduced themselves it became clear that we were a remarkably international group. A rough count then, which was confirmed as the days went by, suggested that there were about twenty five Australians, eight or nine Greeks, five or six Austrians, three or four Brazilians, an Irishman, a Korean and a Japanese; there were only two Britons besides ourselves.

The large number of Australians seemed to confirm what we had already been told about the relationship between that country and the city of Perugia. Evidently an enterprising Australian tour operator had realised that a cheap way to get Australians into Italy was to register them for this course where fees were low, accommodation with local families cheap, and food at the University canteen - *la mensa* - was available for next to nothing. Whether they used their time profitably learning Italian or spent it on trips to Rome, Florence and other tourist attractions was their affair. The twenty five present at that first class soon dwindled, and we concluded that most were here for enjoyment.

What was surprising was that many were second generation Italians whose parents had emigrated to Australia, despite which their young ones had only elementary Italian. We were told by one Australian lady who attended the course faithfully, that acceptance of the young by their Australian peers depended on them becoming whole-hearted Aussies and not clinging to their ethnic background. What a golden opportunity missed to become bilingual.

Our professor proceeded with the first lesson which attempted nothing complex or advanced, raising our morale by leaps and bounds as he did so, and laying an excellent foundation for the weeks to come. He was a good looking man of perhaps fifty years of age, and not the least interesting thing about him was his sartorial elegance. On that first morning he was wearing smart grey trousers, a brownish sports jacket and a snappy yellow waistcoat; his ensemble was completed by a cream shirt, a smart tie and brightly polished shoes.

It was with some surprise, however, when on the second morning he appeared in precisely the same outfit; and when, on the third, this was repeated again it was clear that this was his outfit for the week. Week two found him equally smart but differently attired, whilst week three repeated what we had seen in week one. Only during week four, when our course was approaching its conclusion, was any variation introduced from day to day, and then it was minimal.

His neat attire and charming personality were accompanied by unfailing courtesy. As the days went by he learnt the first names of many of the regular attenders, and addressed them as Elena or Maria or Francesco or Gino, but Hazel was always 'signora' and I was always 'dottore'.

Professor Silvestrini enlivened many of his lectures with a few little jokes - *barzellette* - and these were generally about the *carabiniere*. The *carabiniere*, who are often seen to be driving around in their motorcars, are in reality soldiers, not truly policemen at all. They are surely an excellent body of men, but in many Italian jokes told about them they are represented as very stupid indeed.

'One of them was knocking a nail into a wall,' said the professor, by way of illustrating the meaning of a *barzelletta*, 'but he had the head against the wall and was hitting the point with his hammer. "*Stupido*," cried his superior, arriving at that moment and pointing to the opposite side of the room, "don't you realise that this nail goes into that wall not this one?"'

And the professor illustrated how a carbiniere ties his shoe by putting his left shoe onto a chair and bending down to tie the right one on the floor.

It was all very funny but we never thought them a joke whenever we saw them. From time to time several would come into a shop where we sometimes bought a few things for lunch, but they always looked about seven feet tall, wore massive boots and seemed far too forbidding to be the butt of anyone's jokes.

We were extremely fortunate to have a teacher of Professor Silvestrini's calibre, and equally lucky with his second in command. She was an elegant lady professor - *una professoressa* - called Valeria, and she was the epitome of the dark Italian beauty we see so often. But as a teacher she was superb, more serious, perhaps, than the professor but she introduced the necessary variety into our course with no loss of quality whatever.

Those of us who were regular attenders, perhaps twenty five or so, were kept very busy. Three hours of teaching during the morning was supplemented on some days by afternoon or evening classes in conversation, language laboratory sessions, and other interesting presentations on our subject. Sections of the professor's book had been produced in dramatic form on videotapes, with actors and actresses playing the roles we were following in our books - and every video was introduced by an aria sung by - who else but Pavarotti.

The intellectual challenge of which my colleague in London had spoken was surely there. Each day we returned to the faded luxury of La Dogana satisfied with the intense mental effort we were making. On busy days we were, as the Italians say, *fatica da cane* - tired as dogs - but we enjoyed every bit of it.

Chapter 3

La Campagna
The Countryside

Our first weekend found us more than ready for some relaxation. We had worked hard and enjoyed it thoroughly, but now we were anxious to go out and about and talk to anyone we might meet.

The Umbrian countryside has much to offer and there are far fewer tourists than in Tuscany. Touro where we were now living offered tourists little, but residents, in which cateogory we now regarded ourselves, everything. We established rapport quickly with shopkeepers, newspaper sellers, men in the street, in the church, the bars, in fact, wherever we went.

A short drive out of town took us to the shores of Lake Trasimeno, the fourth largest lake in Italy. It was the scene of battle centuries ago when Hannibal and his elephants passed that way, a battle still remembered in local place names - Sanguineto, recalling the bloodbath and Ossaio, the bones of the dead. Napoleon also passed that way, and is said to have thought about draining the lake. It is in fact, extremely shallow, nowhere more than a few metres deep. The locals fish from flat bottomed boats to catch a variety of fresh water fish about which we knew nothing

- until later we sampled them at an excellent restaurant we discovered.

Not far from the Tuoro end of the lake there are two islands, Isola Maggiore, the larger, and Isola Minore, the smaller. Minore in uninhabited but Maggiore has houses, shops, a restaurant and a lace making industry.

We paid an early visit to Isola Maggiore. The ferry - *il traghetto* - made a number of trips each day from the town of Passignano, a short distance to the east of Tuoro, calling at our tiny landing stage and then going across to the island and back again. The island is encircled by a narrow path which allows a comfortable hour's walk, or longer if one chooses to stand and stare or sit and rest. Not far from the beginning of the path on the eastern side, San Francesco is waiting to meet any travellers who might pass that way.

We passed that way on a beautiful Sunday morning, although it was still early January. A man, with whom we fell into conversation whilst waiting for the *traghetto*, observed that it was just like spring - *come primavera*. In fact the month of January 1991 was like it most of the time and even when it was cold, it was dry and invigorating. We crossed on the ferry with the local priest who travelled over to say Mass there every weekend. On arrival we set off around the western side of the island and soon came upon a larger - than - life statue of San Francesco by the edge of the lake.

The story was that the saint had come to visit the island early in the thirteenth century and a local fisherman had given him a carp. St Francis released it, whereupon the grateful fish followed him about until he gave it his blessing.

The gentle stroll we enjoyed on Isola Maggiore was in sharp contrast to a visit we made to the town of Cortona, just over the Tuscany border. My interest in saints, and the manner in which they are depicted in art, takes us to all sorts of places and I wanted to see the Basilica of Santa Margherita of Cortona. Hazel agreed, as usual, and since we had managed to find a parking place for the car we set off on foot - Shank's pony as we would say, or 'the horse of San Francesco' as they say in Italy. This was a grave error. The hill, at the top of which the Basilica is to be found, is formidable. The fourteen stations of the Cross are placed at long intervals as the path goes higher and higher so that at no time were we in any doubt as to how much further we needed to go. The sixth station found us panting hard, the ninth gasping feebly and we still had five more stations to go. Only when we tottered out onto the piazza before the Basilica did we discover that we could have driven up easily.

Santa Margherita's path to sanctity was an unusual one. As an adolescent she was seduced by a nobleman from Montepulciano, lived with him for ten years and bore him a son. When he was murdered she renounced her previous life, gave away her possessions and was taken in by two ladies in Cortona. Here she led a life of extreme penance and self - denial, even inflicting punishment on herself if she thought that her mortifications were insufficient. Her extraordinary harshness of life and her manifest holiness influenced many, both in Cortona and elsewhere, whilst her name was associated with numerous cures regarded as miraculous. She died in the year 1297 and her body remained incorrupt and is to be seen in the Basilica today.

Our weekends gave us the chance to explore the famous and the lesser known sites of Umbria. We made a second visit to Assisi and to the Hermitage on the slopes of the mountain where St. Francis spent time alone in prayer and contemplation. If the magnificent Basilica in the town of Assisi, built to hold his relics and wonderfully decorated with episodes from his life by Giotto in the year 1230, does not wholly reflect the essence of this holy man, his lonely dwelling on the mountainside does. His spirit is at its most intense here but, in truth, it pervades the whole of Umbria and far beyond.

He was the son of a wealthy cloth maker and, although christened John, he was always known as Francesco - the French one - Perhaps because his mother had come from Provence. As a young man he was captured whilst fighting for Assisi against Perugia and was seriously ill when he was released after more than a year. He later renounced his inheritance and devoted himself to a life of poverty and hardship in the service of God. After a period of living alone as a hermit he was joined by seven disciples who travelled widely with him preaching God's word. At first Francesco's message was not well received, giving rise to the legend of his sermon to the birds, because the people would not listen to him. On returning from these preaching journeys he and his followers lived a simple, communal life in great poverty, praying, carrying out their religious observances and helping the poor and sick. Around the year 1210 the simple rule by which they lived, which later became that of the Franciscan Order, was approved by Rome. With his preaching now receiving greater acceptance, he travelled more widely, even dreaming of the conversion of the Saracens, a vain dream as it turned out, although he did manage to pass through their lines and meet the Sultan. In the year 1224, worn out by hardship and penance, he was praying alone on the summit of Monte La Verna when, in ecstasy, he received the imprint of Christ's wounds on his hands, feet and side, although these were not seen by anyone until after his death in 1226 at the age of 45. A visit to Assisi, tourist centre though it may be, is nonetheless an emotional experience which neither of us will ever forget.

The capture of San Francesco whilst fighting against Perugia is merely one example of the extraordinary aggression between cities and between families within a city which existed in medieval Italy. The notion that Assisi and Perugia, or Florence and Siena, should be at war with each other seems quite astonishing when we remember that, nowadays, Italians are not renowned for their warlike qualities. Such local aggression, our Italian teacher in England tells us, springs from the fierce loyalty which Italians of earlier times had for their home town. The Italian word which describes this local pride is *campanilismo* signifying obsession with the *campanile* of your own church which was regarded as superior to all others. We would call it parochialism carried to an extreme degree, but it is a characteristic which, to some extent, is evident today in smaller Italian towns and villages where local events alone matter and national ones can be forgotten about. There is a saying about it - *moglie e buoi dei paesi tuoi,* which means 'get a wife and an ox from your own town.'

Not far south of Assisi is the hill town of Montefalco, home of St. Clare of Montefalco, so of course I had to go there. Hazel, with memories of Cortona, was less enthusiastic, but agreed. It was a visit to remember for two very different reasons.

The ancient church of San Francesco was no longer in use and had been converted to a museum filled, quite literally, by wall paintings of astonishing beauty. The apse had frescos illustrating episodes from the life of the saint which had been created by Benozzo Gozzoli in the fifteenth century. Other artists from the area had contributed many fine works around the remaining walls of the church.

We were too late to see other churches in Montefalco, which we understood held fine works of art too, but in any event, there is a limit to what we are able to absorb at any one time and the St. Francis museum, with its accompanying picture gallery, had satiated us. However, we did have another treat in store.

Enquiring as we left the museum about restaurants in the town we were told that there were two, one excellent and the other less good, but quite acceptable. The first was catering for a wedding party and could not take us. At the second we stepped down into a large vaulted room which was quite empty, suggesting that the museum lady's estimate of its quality might be correct, but we were hungry and there was a huge inviting blaze in a large range so we took a table indicated by the proprietor and greeted him in our best Italian. It was not, of course, good enough to disguise our foreign origin, since he replied by asking us if we wished to choose something special, or if we would leave it to him. We left it to him gladly and what emerged was quite splendid. I no longer remember all of the details, but I do recall that we began with three dishes which were brought to the table separately;

as we finished one there was another. A raviolone, a risotto with four cheeses and tagliatelle with truffles. I believe we must have had a delicate veal dish followed by a *dolce*, accompanied by a free gift of small glasses of a sweet red wine called, we later learned, Sagrantino Passito, a speciality of the Montefalco region. Sweet red wine is, in our experience, uncommon, but this one was beautiful. During our meal other tables had become occupied and we preferred to think that the occupants were discerning diners, rather than rejects from the wedding party's restaurant.

On another weekend we were again to sample the culinary delights of Umbria. A friend had told us that we must visit the little town of Spello, just east of Assisi and dine at *Il Molino* - The Mill. We had the foresight to reserve a table for Sunday lunch by telephone a few days earlier. Conducting a successful telephone conversation in Italian can raise one's spirits enormously, since one is obliged to understand the replies without the benefit of seeing the expressive gesticulations with which all Italians punctuate their conversation. It was as well that we did.

Spello is a hill town similar to Montefalco but far, far steeper. Only Gubbio, which we had previously visited, and were to visit again, can in our experience, compete with it. Climbing the near vertical roads in our rental car was a feat in itself and finding a parking place was even greater

one. As we approached *Il Molino*, we noticed a
steady stream of well dressed Italians approaching
it as well, and it became clear that people came
to this restaurant from far and wide. No wonder.

Every detail of the meal we consumed at Il
Molino can no longer be recalled clearly but the
recollection of its high quality remains very much
alive. It was a large restaurant with a gigantic open
fire in the middle of one wall to which waiters
and waitresses brought what seemed to be a never
ending stream of cuts of meat of different kinds,
all of which were grilled over the hot embers by
a small, fat Italian lady who, perspiring freely
from the intense heat before her, thrust pairs of
large griddles, which grasped ten or twelve steaks
or whatever, into the fire. So far as we could tell,
all the meat consumed in that restaurant, and
there was a great deal of it, was cooked by her.
Hazel could not resist going over to congratulate
her as we left.

The little town of Spello offered us another
treat. The Church of Santa Maria Maggiore,
almost next door to *Il Molino*, contained frescos
and an Annunciation by Pintoricchio. There was
also an attractive floor made of antique majolica
tiles from nearby Deruta. That Sunday lives on
in memory.

And so does an expedition we made into the
south of Umbria to Orvieto. Since our
enjoyment of wine exceeds even that of churches,
we felt that we had to visit Orvieto, which

produces such excellent white wine. The road to Orvieto out of Perugia is a fast dual carriageway for most of its length, which takes one past the little town of Deruta - or might have done if we had not seen the tiles on the floor of Santa Maria Maggiore in Spello. Even if we had not intended to visit there the majolica ware, which locals hang on the walls of their houses backing onto the main road, might have enticed us in.

The Italian word for majolica is, fortunately, *maiolica*, whilst that for ceramics is *ceramiche*. I suppose there must be a difference but we have yet to learn what it is. On several occasions we have been on the point of asking but we have always refrained, mainly because, if the explanation turned out to be a technical one, as we expected it would, we might not be able to understand it in Italian.

There was no doubt, however, that whichever we meant to buy, Deruta was the place to buy it. After all, Deruta is the most famous ceramics centre in Umbria, possibly in Italy, and the population have been producing their wonderful work for centuries.

When there are shops by the score, or even by the hundred, how does one choose where to take one's custom? Our choice was arbitrary and determined by nothing more than a ready availability of a parking place outside one of the early shops we saw; it was a fortunate choice, nevertheless. The shop - lady was happy to talk to us - as indeed were almost all the Italians we met - and she showed us different patterns, colours and sizes before leaving us to wander. The problem of what kind of present to take back to England for the family is easily solved in Deruta; everybody gets *ceramiche* (or *maiolica.*) If one is fortunate to get as cooperative a sales - lady as we did, you may even get a *sconto* - discount - as we did. Since Deruta *majolica* (or *ceramiche*) is less expensive in Deruta than elsewhere, we were delighted with the deal we got and promised to come again, as we did, more than once.

Orvieto, surmounting, as so many Italian towns and cities do, a steep hill, has much to offer but nothing so splendid as its *Duomo.* This cathedral, started in the thirteenth century, worked on by various master architects and hundreds of ordinary stone masons, is a thing of outstanding beauty. The striking colour of the mosaics on its facade meets the eye instantly; the details of its remarkable sculptures are beyond belief. The story of the bible is told in stone from the creation of the world to the day of judgement and the symbols of the four evangelists, a winged man, ox, lion and eagle cast in bronze project proudly out onto the piazza. Sadly, to carry this masterpiece away on a colour photograph is difficult since the piazza itself does not allow a sufficiently distant view.

Within the *Duomo* looks, at first, gloomy but with the illumination provided for tourists by coin meters, the dazzling frescos of the 'Capella della Madonna di San Brizio,' started by Fra Angelico and continued by other masters in later years, becomes evident in all its beauty.

If there is a more beautiful building than this in the whole of Italy, we have yet to see it. We came to the country to learn more of the language but we needed no language at all to enjoy the magnificence before us.

Despite the extra accommodation in our apartment, we had only one guest during our stay. Our elder son, who was skiing in France, made the long journey to spend the weekend with us. He is both an excellent cook and a wine buff so we had to find something special to meet his needs.

To satisfy his urge for high quality wine, we chose to go to Montepulciano in Tuscany. Here they have an exceptional wine with a resounding name - *Vino Nobile di Montepulciano*, the noble wine of Montepulciano. Years ago detractors, no doubt from other vineyards in other regions, had claimed that the Vino Nobile was so called only because, when first produced, it was drunk solely by the aristocracy. Such base aspersions can be dismissed as, literally, sour grapes - *uve acide* by anyone who samples this excellent wine, as we did that morning.

There was something for me too in Montepulciano - two things in fact. It is one of those splendid, ancient hill towns of Tuscany where just to stroll the streets is to feel that you have gone back in time hundreds of years. If one is lucky in one of those marvellous old towns, one may occasionally come across a wall painting, perhaps of the virgin and child or the patron saint of the town or region, on the side of a house. Some of these are almost too weathered by sun, rain and wind to be discernable, but a few survive, like that of St. Jerome which we found that day in a back street. Jerome was a great scholar - it was he who produced a Latin text of the bible we call the Vulgate - and in art he is usually shown pouring over his books in his study with a lion lying beside him; the unlikely story being that he once removed a thorn from its foot and it became his devoted servant thereafter. At any event, there they were, Jerome and his lion, gazing upon the three of us from the side of a house in Montepulciano.

This painting, beautiful though it was, could not compare with one of St. Eligius we had seen some years earlier on a wall in Sirmione, beside the shores of Lake Garda. Eligius is the Patron Saint of Blacksmiths and the painting showed him shoeing a horse in a novel fashion - for easier working he had taken off its back leg, which he later replaced!

My second treat that day was to visit the elegant basilica of San Biagio - whom we in England call St. Blaise. It lies in the valley outside the town and it is approached along a fine avenue of cypress trees, each with a marker to commemorate a soldier who died in World War I. It is a splendid, symmetrical building with a graceful campanile and a wonderful marble interior. San Biagio, for whom it was named, is a special favourite of mine. He was bishop of Sebaste, in Armenia, around the fourth century and was a great healer of animals as well as man. His first patient was a boy who had a bone stuck in his throat; San Biagio cured him and became the patron saint of throats.

To escape one of the Christian prosecutions of that time he fled to the mountains where he continued his healing activities. He was finally found when hunters, seeking animals to fight in the ampitheatre, were attracted to his cell by the concentrations of animals gathered there. He was put in prison in total darkness until an old woman, whose pig he saved from a wolf, brought him candles. This story has a modern application for, when throats are blessed on his feast day, February third, crossed candles are held in front of the throat as the blessing is said. They say that Placido Domingo prays every day to San Biagio - and no wonder.

After a diet of saints and *vino nobile* we needed a diet of another kind. My excellent guide book told me that south of Montepulciano, in the town of Chiusi, there was an exceptional restaurant - so exceptional that Italians who were 'in the know,' who were travelling down the autostrada between Rome and Florence would turn off the road to dine at Zaira in the old town. It was indeed very fine but, like all restaurants with a high reputation, everyone speaks English. Back to the tavernas for us in the future.

Chapter 4

Ancora La Scuola
Back to School

The remaining weeks of our course continued in the same efficient way in which it had begun. The book we were using was set out as a series of little stories, with details of the grammatical points illustrated and amplified in various exercises which followed.

In these lessons sundry characters were seen visiting Assisi and having a picnic - *un pranzo al sacco* - or being interviewed for a job. One young man was watching a mystery story on the TV - *un giallo,* called this because such books are produced with a yellow cover - but the identity of the assassin remained unknown, since the young man fell asleep and when he woke up the TV was showing an advertisement for ladies' stockings. There was a birthday party where everyone sang *Tanti Auguri a Te* - Happy Birthday to You - to the same tune that we use. Far less pleasant was a visit to the dentist in which the dental drill - *il trapino* - figured largely. The actors in the videos, who were portraying what we were reading, were most realistic and we quickly became familiar with Pavarotti's aria, which introduced each episode. Since every story illustrated some aspect of grammar, like the present, past or future or, as in later lessons, the subjective - *il congiuntivo* - common in Italy but little used in English, this was an excellent way to learn. Had our English grammar not been long forgotten we might have done better, but we did feel that we were keeping our end up and, hopefully, improving.

In fact, we did have an advantage over some of the other nationals who were attending the course, one which we had not previously appreciated. We realised that, from time to time, one of the class would be ignorant of a word which to us had an obvious meaning; *confusione,* for example, which to anyone from Britain clearly meant confusion. *Informazione* means information, *interessante* could only be interesting. Who could have any difficulty in translating from Italian into English the phrase *respirazione artificiale.* Such similarity no doubt sprang from a common Latin origin and the similarity might not be evident in say Greek, German or Portuguese and certainly not in Korean of Japanese. One had to modify pronunciation from time to time, but after a while this became fairly simple. The long 'i' of 'fragile,' for instance, is pronounced as would be the short 'i' of 'illusion' and the final 'e' takes on a sound like 'eh' so that the word emerges as something like 'frageeleh.' 'Acrobat' becomes 'acrobato' with both 'o's accented and 'TV' is 'TVoo.' There was always the possibility of a different meaning too, despite a superficial similarity in the words themselves; the use of the word *costipazione* need not necessarily be considered inelegant, since its Italian meaning is 'stuffed up' or 'catarrhal'.

Concentrating so hard, as we did, on the language that we were trying to learn had the unusual effect of driving any other foreign language completely out of our minds. Whenever we tried to think of a French word, for example, only its Italian equivalent came up. One morning we received a message from our eldest son, who was skiing in France, asking us to ring him. Throughout lunch that day we struggled to find a suitable French phrase to use, should our call be answered by a French-speaking person at the other end. Having finally, and with great difficulty, found what we thought would do, our call was answered by a very English chalet girl.

The month of January might have been like spring much of the time, but it was sometimes cold. Moreover the spring-like weather outside the thick stone walls of the University did not penetrate within and we were both suffering from the chill - *come un freddo cane* - like a cold dog, as the Italian phrase has it. We sat solemnly in two jerseys, as much underwear as we could manage and thick socks and boots in an effort to keep warm. From time to time we even tried writing in gloves. Our teachers, who did not seem to mind the cold, were either used to it or wore thermal underwear.

The members of our class began to take on identities of their own. We became friendly with a charming Australian lady, one of the few to stay the course, as well as an Irish priest who had spent some years in Brazil and was fluent in Portuguese. Our small group which had been formed for conversation also contained an English electrician working in the north of Italy, where many people spoke German. There was a young Austrian girl who worked in her father's wood factory, which did a lot of business in Italy, and two Greek boys hoping to get into an Italian University.

We had wondered how two old fogeys like ourselves might be received in a class composed largely of young people. I imagine that they must have regarded us as a curious couple, but not for one moment did we feel that we were other than wholly accepted into the class. As one gets older, if one is wise, one seeks the company of the young; nothing can make you younger, but the company of youngsters, keen to learn as we were, made us feel so.

We were meeting some charming people in the University, in Tuoro and in the countryside on our weekend jaunts, but were we learning anything? We hoped so and the Professor was kind enough to say that we were very good and that we should be in a higher class; but then I have already said that he was a most courteous man!

The Gulf War broke out half way through our course, although it had no influence on our studies. We were, however, somewhat nearer the field of conflict and a few telephone calls home were needed to allay anxiety. Were these two old people alright, on their own in a foreign country at a time like this? We were able to reassure our young ones that we were and went back to the books.

The war did make us read the Italian newspapers more fully and regularly than we had before, to keep up with what was happening. It was evident that the war was, by and large, an unpopular thing among the Italians we met. We had, for example, been in the habit of having lunch in a nearby taverna where a bright little waitress with a happy smile and cheerful disposition served us daily. The decision to send some Italian soldiers to the Gulf area reduced poor Wanda to tears. She kept on repeating *i ragazzi, i ragazzi* - the young men, the young men - all of whom she clearly felt were going to be in mortal danger.

A period of military service was, and still is, compulsory for young Italian men, unless they are conscientious objectors, in which case they work on the land or in some other non-violent capacity. None of these young conscripts had ever thought they might have to fight.

On another day we were held up behind a silent march for peace in nearby Maggione, whilst prayers for peace were said every evening in the Parish church in Tuoro. Our best opportunity for learning of the intensity of feeling, amongst some of the Italians at least, was the conversation we had with two gentlemen at the town of Castilione del Lago, an elegant medieval town sitting on a rocky promontory on the western shore of lake Trasimeno.

We were watching a game of *boccia*, the precise rules of which we have yet to learn, when we began to talk to our two friends. It became evident that there was considerable opposition to the war in which Britain was directly involved. With true Italian courtesy, however, no criticism of Britain's part was expressed at the time, whatever they may have said later in private.

The game of *boccia*, which we have found fascinating every time we have visited Italy, has some similarity to bowls but the balls used, two or four to a player, have no bias. Any curving motion from right or left is imparted by cunning twists of the wrist. The game is invariably accompanied by shouts of encouragement and abuse at the top of the players voices, especially when, as happens frequently, the last player takes deadly aim and fires in his ball with all his strength to scatter several of his opponents' balls, which are in a winning position. The game was instantly intriguing to us both, but alas, it had its sad side. Although we watched *boccia* on that afternoon - or more correctly, in Italian terminology, that evening, since the evening - *la sera* - starts soon after the midday meal - and at other times over the years, we never succeeded in deciphering a single word uttered by the over excited players, which was a serious blow to our linguistic pride.

From our regular reading of the newspapers we learned of an opportunity we could not allow to go by. We usually read *La Repubblica,* which each week published a colour supplement. During our second week at the University this dealt with the famous artist Piero della Francesca, so called because his father died before he was born and, as a result, he was given his mother's name. He had been born in the northern Umbrian town of Sansepolcro at some time between 1410 and 1420, the precise date being unknown. He died in the year 1492. Preparations were being made for his 500th anniversary in twelve months time.

Sansepolcro was scarcely fifty kilometres from Tuoro so, on the following Saturday we set out there to visit the house of his birth, now the Museo Civico, which had several of his most famous canvasses and others by his renowned pupil, Luca Signorelli. There were two included amongst many of great beauty which were nothing short of magnificent. The first was of the resurrection, which showed Christ emerging from His tomb, about to stride over four sleeping guards. It is a stark picture with a brown and bare landscape behind Jesus, but it is mesmerising in its powerful message. The second picture of special note is called the 'Misericordia Polyptych'. It is an enormous altarpiece showing a small crucifixion scene at its apex, below which is a far larger majestic Madonna, holding her cloak open with both hands to shelter beneath it the members of the community who had commissioned the painting. This striking central panel is flanked on each side by saints, whilst below are scenes of Christ's final agonies, burial, resurrection and empty tomb.

There was one further picture of the Madonna, of which we had been informed by La Repubblica, but to see this masterpiece we had to leave the city of Sansepolcro and drive a short distance south to the tiny village of Monterchi. We were to look for a little chapel, we had been told, but it took some time to find. Eventually we drove up a narrow lane to a *cappella* so tiny that the picture, when we saw it, occupied the entire far wall where once the altar had been. This painting is, we believe, unique, being the only one in existence which shows the Virgin Mary in the last month of her pregnancy. She bares a striking resemblance, as well she might, to the Madonna in the Misercordia

Polyptych, but this time two angels are pulling aside a curtain to reveal her, serene and magnificent in a blue gown which, in view of her advanced pregnancy, cannot be quite closed across the upper part of her abdomen; here she holds her right hand as though trying to bring the edges together. The masterpiece is called *La Madonna del Parto* and for me it had special significance.

We greatly enjoyed our weekend jaunts into the Italian countryside, but we returned to the University each Monday ready for whatever our teachers had in store for us. It is an art to make every lecture interesting and that is what Professor Silvestrini did. He began one week by mentioning the Italian phrase *'Meglio un ouvo oggi che una gallina domani'* - literally, 'better an egg today than a hen tomorrow', expressing much the same view as 'a bird in the hand is worth two in the bush'. He used several other phrases during his lecture and we became fascinated by the similarities as well as the differences between the sayings of our two countries.

There are many which are almost exactly the same, such as,

'Chi non s'avventura non ha ventura' - 'nothing ventured, nothing gained.'

'Cascare dalla pedela nella braca' - 'out of the frying pan, into the fire.'

'Non svegliare il can che dorme' - 'let sleeping dogs lie.'

'*Via la gatta, i topi ballano*' - 'when the cat's away the mice will play.'

Others had a similar meaning with somewhat different imagery.

'*Quattro occhi valgono piu di due*' - 'four eyes are worth more than two' - or, as we would put it, '*two heads are better than one.*'

'*Essere sano come un pesce*' - To be as 'fit as a fish' or a fiddle as way we say.

'*Una rondine non fa primavera.*' - 'one swallow does not make a spring', or summer, as we would express it. When one thinks about it, swallows would be expected to arrive much sooner in Italy than in England.

'*Prendere due piccione con una fava*' - 'take two pigeons with a bean' - a rather mystifying expression signifying 'to kill two birds with one stone.'

The most interesting of all to us were the expressions which conveyed a similar meaning to our English ones but in totally different terms.

'Once bitten twice shy' appears as '*Cane scottata dall'acqua calda ha paura della fredda*', meaning literally 'a dog scalded by hot water is afraid of cold.'

'Don't cross a bridge before you come to it' is reflected by '*non si fasci la testa prima di averla rotta*', which means 'don't bandage your head until you have broken it.'

'Give him an inch and he will take a yard' becomes '*se gli da un dito si prende il braccio,*' literally 'if you give him a finger he will take an arm.'

'He was born with a silver spoon in his mouth' is *'e nato con la camicia'* or, 'he was born in a shirt.'

'Between the devil and the deep blue sea' is *'Fra l'incudine e il martello,'* or 'between the anvil and the hammer.'

Finally one with a special Italian flavour is the phrase for 'once in a blue moon,' is *'ad ogni morte di Papa,'* which is 'at every death of the Pope,' arising from the notion that popes do not resign, but go on until they drop.

Another subject we found full of interest was that of Italian superstition. Surprisingly in an intensely religious country superstition is widespread. Many, for example, still firmly believe in the evil eye - *il malocchio.* Others cherish the notion that a deceased grandparent will appear to them in a dream to tell them the winning numbers in the national lottery or the winning combination for the football pool - *il totocalcio.* Ideas of witches and magicians - *steghe e maghi* - are by no means things of the past, whilst almost any newspaper or magazine you pick up will have an important section devoted to horoscopes. It was interesting to us, after finding so many Italian idioms and sayings with different imagery, that many supposedly unlucky things are the same in our two countries. Admittedly an Italian would 'touch iron' - *tocca ferro* - instead of wood for good luck, but that apart, there are many similarities. An Italian will cross his fingers - *fare le corni* make the horns - to ward off evil. He would consider it the height of folly to walk under a ladder and if he were unfortunate enough to have a black cat cross the street in front of him this would be the worst possible luck. And who would ever run the risk of opening an umbrella in the house? Of course, the only way to ward off misfortune after spilling salt is to take a little of it and throw it over your shoulder.

But no Italian would be concerned about the number thirteen; for him or her seventeen is the unlucky number.

It was all fascinating, but of course, it had come to an end. Without a doubt, it had been a marvellous experience and we were both agreed that we must come again at the end of the year. Next time we would be able to live in the city. Emanuele and Paola owned an apartment there which they rarely used and it could be ours for the month of November. So we said our goodbyes to our teachers, packed our bags and headed for home.

But before we left, we were offered a certificate of attendance if we wished it - Lire 10,000!

Chapter 5

Perugia

January 1991 might have been *come primavera* but November was undoubtedly winter - *l' inverno.*

We drove down from Bologna in another Fiat Uno, in the pouring rain, to meet Emanuele, who led the way in his pick up truck into the city of Perugia. Feeling superior because we now knew our way around the city, we followed him to a narrow street off a small piazza only a short distance from the Palazzo Galengo. We would be able to walk there in three or four minutes.

Number fourteen, Via Guardabassi was an old apartment block of three floors; we were on the second. We parked our car temporarily, half on the pavement and half off it whilst we unloaded. As we made our way up the two flights of stone steps, Emanuele explained various things he thought we ought to know. The significance of one of them rang a tiny warning bell at the back of my mind, and then I dismissed it, as he went on to explain something else. What he had done was to open the door of a small compartment in the wall outside the front door and indicate that we could turn off the water there if we needed to.

The flat was spacious, not by La Dogana standards, but ample for the two of us. There was a entrance hall, a large lounge with a TV set, a good sized bedroom and a second smaller one. There were two bathrooms, one beside the bedrooms and the other, surprisingly, by the front door. The former was a newly tiled modern bathroom with a large bath and shower, whilst the latter contained a short tub into which one could, with some difficulty, climb and sit with knees drawn up in the fetal position, since the floor of the tub was at two levels.

Emanuele told us that we would not be able to park our car outside the flat or even near it; only residents with their cars were allowed to do that, visitors with rental cars were obliged to go elsewhere. 'Elsewhere' proved to be some distance away, not horizontally but vertically. After driving downhill through exceedingly narrow streets I came to a car park which was largely empty, it being Sunday night, where I could leave the car all week for nothing. I did not have to walk all the way back uphill; two long escalators - *scale moblili* - brought me up from the car park, almost as far as the flat. The *Perugini* had clearly utilised every modern convenience to cope with their steep hills. With accommodation such as we had, close to the Palazzo Galengo and the food and wine shops immediately opposite the flat, we felt that we were well organised.

L' iscrizione on the Monday morning was a very pleasant surprise. This time we were well prepared with several photographs, photocopies of our passports and two stamps bought that morning before we entered the palazzo. This time there was no confusion, no jostling crowds of students, no panic. The whole process, *polizia* and all, was over in less than thirty minutes. Only then did we realise that our registration in January had been so traumatic because everyone was registering then - students who were coming only for a month and those who were coming for three, six or twelve months. We could scarcely have picked a worse time to come.

Our elation at the simplicity of registration was quickly dashed when we were told that our class, now level three - *livello tre* - would not be held in the Palazzo Galengo but in another building some distance away. Instead of a three or four minutes stroll in the mornings, we were faced with a much longer and far more complicated trudge through the city to our new classroom. Our journey each day took us up into the Piazza del Duomo, out of its far corner, into and out of a market where clothes, shoes, wallets, umbrellas and livestock of all kinds were sold, down two flights of steps, down again in a large outside elevator, across the busy traffic at the mouth of the Galleria Kennedy and down, down, down to relatively modern buildings where we were to be taught. Coming back, which we sometimes did twice a day, was far more exhausting.

This time we were a small class, perhaps twenty five in all, but generally fewer; fifteen or sixteen. We were as international a group as on our previous visit but with no Australians, several more Greeks, a German lady, a Brazilian, an English boy and girl and a Croatian, who was no doubt delighted to escape the horrors which were being perpetrated in his country at the time. Our new professor was far from the fashion plate Professor Silvestrini had been. Professor Mencacci wore a crumpled suit and no tie but he knew how to teach. He began his first lesson with the *passato remoto* - past definite.

In Italian there are three different ways of referring to something done in the past. If that something still has some relevance to the present day, the tense to use is present perfect. If the event in the past was a continuous one or a recurrent one, like 'he was doing' or 'everyday he used to,' the appropriate tense is the imperfect. Both of these tenses we were familiar with, not exactly fluent in, but familiar with. The *passato remoto* was a different matter and could be used to refer to an event in the past which no longer had any relevance to the present.

The professor illustrated this tense to us with an example from Dante Alighieri. Dante, as we call him, is always given his full name by Italians and is held in little short of veneration by many of them. This was especially so in Perugia since some of his masterpiece - *Il Suo Capolavoro* - was written there. This is how the professor explained it. Dante Alighieri wrote the 'Divine Comedy' - *'La Divina Commedia'*. This was an event of immense importance then and still is, hence we use the present perfect - *L'ha scritto* - he wrote it.

For Dante Alligieri was writing when a friend called to see him (continuous action) or used to write every afternoon (repetitive action) we use the imperfect - *scriveva* - he was writing.

But 'Dante Alligieri sneezed' is of no importance now, hence we use the *passato remoto* - *starnutò* - he sneezed.

Unfortunately the *passato remoto* is a complicated tense and for many verbs it is highly irregular. These were difficult classes but we needed to get to grips with it, since it is used widely in Italian writing. Strangely, it is scarcely ever used in conversation in the north of Italy, but is frequently used in the south.

We battled on in our attempts to use these three constructions correctly, but as we look back over some of the exercises we did then, we were often wrong - and still are.

This time the age difference between the next oldest person in the class and ourselves was somewhat less, since the German and Brazilian ladies had a maturity not evident in anyone in our January class. With the ready acceptance we had received in January, we were less conscious of our seniority this time. Learning a foreign language at an advanced age is not easy, because things fade from the memory more quickly - even immediately, except for events of long ago. It must have been about this time that Hazel first used a phrase which we often think of still - *capisco ma non mi ricordo* - I understand but I can't remember.

Perhaps age does have some compensations, a concept neatly referred to in the Italian phrase *gallina vecchia fa buon brodo* - literally 'an old hen makes good soup', suggesting that an older person is often worth more than a younger one, due to age and experience. We sometimes comforted ourselves with this notion when the going got tough, conveniently overlooking the fact that the phrase is sometimes jokingly used about a young man who marries a woman older than himself.

At number fourteen, Via Gaurdabassi, the need to bathe in the tub in the fetal position became a reality all too soon. The water from the hot tap in our splendid modern bathroom remained cold even after it had been running for ten minutes, though the water in the second bathroom was pleasantly warm. There was nothing for it but to clamber over the steep side of the tub and wash in a cramped sitting position. This disturbed Hazel more than me, not because she was less agile, but because her idea of heaven is to lie stretched out in a bath reading a book. Reading in the tub was definitely out.

We soon became aware of other shortcomings of the flat. The refrigerator was so cold that it froze the milk in its container. Some prosciutto, bought that morning from the shop across the street, was stiff by lunch time. Our fridge had become a *congelatore* in the true sense of the word, congealing everything within it to a near inedible state. No amount of fiddling decreased its temperature and we were reduced to trying to find the least cold part, which turned out to be the vegetable compartment.

The problem that we encountered on our first Sunday was much more serious. I was shaving quietly in our secondary bathroom when I heard a steady drip, drip, drip behind me; the boiler had sprung a leak. A basin put underneath to catch the drips, which were now increasing almost to a steady stream, seemed likely to become full all too soon. Since we planned a jaunt out into the country the water would have to be turned off. We recalled Emanuele's words, as he pointed to the cupboard on the landing on our arrival, saying that this was where we could turn the water off if necessary.

We rang La Dogana with no success. Emanuele was away in Rome and would not be back until Monday morning. Paola knew nothing about boilers and neither did we. The water would just have to go on when we needed it and off when we didn't. We would hope for the best.

Our problem at La Dogana had been the shower - *la doccia*, now it was the drip - *la goccia*.

In the long run the leak proved to be an advantage. Emanuele produced a plumber - *un idraulico* - early on Monday, and that worthy fellow not only fixed the leak but got hot water through to our beautiful new bathroom as well. Hazel heaved a sigh of relief and began to get through her paper backs at a brisker rate.

Our next problem arose during our second week, just as we were thinking that our troubles might be behind us. Because we were to be in the flat for only a month we had arranged with Emanuele that a lady should come in once or twice to clean. On her first morning this poor lady switched on the vacuum cleaner - *l' aspirapolvere* - and fused most of the lights in the flat except for our bedroom. That evening we sat solemnly in our bedroom awaiting the arrival of Emanuele, who had told us about everything in the flat except where to find the fuse box. What, we wondered, would happen next?

We did not have long to wait. On the Sunday of our second weekend it was exceedingly wet - so wet in fact that the torrential rain drove straight through the roof of our small bathroom. Soon there was one, two, three and finally four leaks. The apartment had only one bucket but we found a large bowl and two big saucepans to catch the drips as best we could; *le goccie* were after us again. This time there was nothing Emanuele could do, so we had to empty the containers at intervals and wait for the rain to stop. It did so around lunch time but we were loath to go far, and our outing that day was seriously curtailed.

Problems are supposed to come in threes and we had had four; might this perhaps be the end? We hoped so and touched wood; for luck we touched iron as well - *tocca ferro*, which is what an Italian would have done.

Touching iron evidently did the trick and we remained trouble free in the apartment from then on. We still had a frozen refrigerator to deal with but apart from that we were comfortable. We had an otherwise satisfactory kitchen; we occasionally ate at home in the evenings, more then we had originally envisaged. There were several good butchers nearby and my wife's cooking is in par with, if not better than, whatever the best Perugian restaurant could produce. We became quite attached to a wine sold by our grocer across the street; the green wine of Jesi. It proved admirable for making one forget the problems of the *passato remoto*. Mostly we ate out, however, and we had a far wider choice of restaurants than we had in Tuoro.

We had reason to be grateful to the proprietor of one restaurant which we visited several times. One Thursday morning, when we were about to leave the flat, I realised that I did not have my wallet, nor could I recall when I had used it last. It seemed possible that I had left it in the restaurant two nights before, but I could not be sure and, in truth, it could have been lost anywhere. The restaurant would not be open until mid - morning or later in any case, so the first thing to do was telephone England to cancel my credit cards. As soon as our mornings work was over we went around to the restaurant and were handed the wallet by a smiling waiter before we had to ask for it. There is a prevailing view that Italians will steal anything that isn't nailed down, but this has not been our experience in Perugia, nor in any of the small towns and villages we had visited.

We were lucky, or I was, that Hazel had an excellent set of credit cards on which we existed for the remainder of our stay.

We found some of the Italian TV interesting but for certain programmes, like dubbed American films, there was something lacking. Lieutenant Columbo translated into Italian and spoken by a voice which bore no resemblance to the self effacing American accent of the 'lootenant' wasn't quite the same. News programmes were useful to improve our comprehension of spoken Italian and we were fascinated by a two hour long programme which advertised for missing persons. Photographs of the missing person were shown, appeals made by relatives and friends and everything got quite emotional. Of course, there was always football - *il calcio* - even, on a couple of occasions, English football. And why not? If we can watch Italian football on television in England, why should not an Italian watch English football in Italy? One who did so regularly commented favourably on it, not however, on the skill but on the commitment and the direct approach. I was never sure if this was a compliment or not.

Our weekend trips were to some extent curtailed by the weather, but we did manage a return visit to Deruta and another to Gubbio. We have always enjoyed Gubbio despite the fact that it has the steepest streets of any town we have ever visited - including Spello. On this visit we found a strange anomaly we had not noticed before. There is a story to it which goes like this:

In the early thirteenth century Gubbio was terrorised by a savage wolf. San Francesco, learning of this, was determined to put matters right. Disregarding warnings for his safety, he searched for and found the beast, addressed it as Brother Wolf, pointed out the error of its ways and brought it back, docile and submissive, to the town.

The event is recalled today by a plaque which has been set up on the spot where the encounter is supposed to have taken place. The mystery - *il mistero* - is this: The plaque commemorating the spot refers to *la pericolosa lupa* - the dangerous she wolf! Why would the saint address a she wolf as Brother Wolf? Did he perhaps not know the difference? I have often wondered.

Despite the poor weather I was anxious to visit two towns in the south east of Umbria; Norcia and Cascia, famous for the saints who lived there.

Norcia, which has become Nursia in English, was the birthplace of a pair of the more famous of the world's twins, Saints Benedict and Scholastica. Benedict, widely regarded as the father of western monasticism did not evolve his famous rule in Norcia but in Subiaco and later in Monte Cassino. He, the more celebrated of the two, is commemorated by the Church of San Benedetto, which was built over the house where the twins were born almost 1,500 years ago. He is also remembered by a large statue in the piazza which also bears his name. He, and his rather overshadowed sister, are both commemorated in a tiny chapel in the crypt of the church.

Norcia is not only a centre of sanctity, but a centre of gastronomic excellence. Wonderfully exotic foods are to be seen hanging outside the numerous food stores in the town; there are truffles, cheeses, wild boar hams and even, though we were not tempted to sample them, wild boar testicles. Hazel made a few vain attempts to obtain a recipe for their preparation, purely out of culinary curiosity and not with any intention of serving them to me.

Benedict is renowned throughout the world, but the next saint we visited, quite literally, is virtually unknown outside of Italy, where she is held in high esteem as the Patron Saint of the impossible. The story of Santa Rita of Cascia is a fascinating one.

Santa Rita lived during the late fourteenth and first half of the fifteenth centuries in a tiny village just outside Cascia. She was a married woman with two sons and a loutish husband. When they died Rita managed, after several attempts, to enter a convent in Cascia where a number of curious events took place. Chief amongst these was the appearance on her forehead of the marks of the crown of thorns like those on the head of Christ. In that sense Rita was a most unusual type of stigmatic since, amongst stigmatics, such crown of thorns marks are a rarity. Even more rare was their suppuration; I know of only one other instance where this has occurred. The wounds became so unpleasant that she was told that, unless they disappeared, she would not be able to go to the 1450 jubilee celebrations in Rome. They cleared up immediately only to reappear on her return. Perhaps this is why Italians regard her as the Patron Saint of the impossible. Like Santa Margherita, whom we met at Cortina earlier, Rita's body also remained incorrupt and is to be seen in a huge Basilica built in recent times to her memory.

This south east corner of Umbria has two large national parks and in one, just to the east of Norcia, is a fascinating natural feature called the Piano Grande. This is a vast flat plain in the middle of a range of mountains and, we are told, is exceptionally beautiful in spring when it becomes a mass of colour with flowers blooming everywhere. In November, in the rain, it still has a majestic appearance, in a desolate kind of way. We had no alternative but to sit in the car and eat our prosciutto - wild boar prosciutto of course which has a special flavour all its own. The desolation of Piano Grande that day added to the mournful sight of the nearby ghost town of Castelluccio, from which ninety percent of the inhabitants departed in recent times. High above the Piano Grande it is truly a *zona isolata* - an isolated place - frequently cut off completely in winter. It is easy to see why it was deserted.

The trip to Piano Grande was our last journey of any distance outside Perugia, not only because of the weather but because we encountered that ubiquitous aspect of Italian life; the strike - *lo sciopero*. Strikes seem to spring up everywhere in Italy and pickets appear on the street as if magic. This *sciopero* was at petrol stations so, having obtained a full tank shortly before the strike began and needing most of it to be sure of getting back to Bologna to catch the plane back to England, we let discretion be the better part of valour and stayed in the city.

Disappointing though this was, it had the advantage that we now had more opportunity to see what Perugia itself had to offer. It is a pleasant city with spacious piazzas, majestic old buildings and an admirable art gallery - La Galleria Nazionale dell' Umbria. Close by the gallery there is a most beautiful fountain, which was designed in the thirteenth century to hold water from the city aqueduct - *La Fontana Maggiore.* The Cathedral of San Lorenzo stands beside this fountain, but has no great artistic merit, although it does claim to possess no less a treasure than the wedding ring of the Virgin Mary! Fifteen separate keys, kept by fifteen different citizens, lock it safely away.

There is a splendid main thoroughfare, the Corso Vanucci where, in the evenings, the citizens engage in one of Italy's favourite pastimes; strolling up and down, meeting ones friends and talking - always talking. In a capital city everyone is dressed in the height of fashion. Elegant shops line both sides of this lovely street and one can drink coffee, sip wine, eat ice cream or buy expensive clothes - Hazel gave me a present of a pair of elephant skin gloves - or one can just watch the world go by.

The Corso Vanucci comes to an end at a wide marble parapet from which one can look way,

way down to the less fashionable parts of the city below. And there is a secret way to reach these distant parts - the subterranean passage beloved of all schoolboys or more correctly, a subterranean town. Centuries ago, during one of the more bloody episodes in Perugia's turbulent past, parts of the city were destroyed by Papel order and other buildings constructed on the site. A change in the city's fortunes many years later led to these newer structures being destroyed in their turn, but parts of the old town beneath, from which the citizens had been driven out, remained. They are still to be seen today; the empty streets and squares of a medieval town, now used only as a thoroughfare. A mobile staircase leads down from the Corso Vanucci to the beginning of the old town, whilst from its lowest part more mobile staircases carry the Perugini about their business up and down each day.

During the long journey to school most mornings we bought a newspaper. In January we had the Gulf War to follow; now we had the mysterious disappearance of Robert Maxwell. There is naturally a good deal of national news in Italian newspapers, but Maxwell drove at least some of this off the front pages for a while, while attempts were being made to find out what had happened. Hazel's task, as soon as we arrived in our classroom, was to read out the latest speculation about the mystery. It was, in Italy at least, a nine days wonder - *un fuoco di paglia* - fire of straw. We had to wait until we returned home to find out the truth of it all.

Our new classroom was bright and airy and, mercifully, nothing like so cold as the Palazzo Galengo, and there was plenty of room to dry umbrellas in the corner. We did miss the Bar Roma. We were near no shops and our morning cappuccino had to come from a little coffee bar in the building itself with, sad to say, some loss in quality.

The last two weeks of our instruction at the university were, in some ways, a disappointment. Our professor had been called away, we knew not where, and his deputy was less successful in teaching us what we needed to know. Whether this was the inexperience of the teacher or the subject matter we were tackling, we cannot be sure but it is true that no teacher since has succeeded in getting us to master Italian prepositions.

Italian prepositions, in our view, defy rational analysis. There seems to be no rhyme or reason in them or, as the Italian phrase goes, they seem to have neither head nor tail - *non avere ne capo ne coda*. A few examples, and these are easy ones, can illustrate the problem.

Going in a motor car is *in macchina*; fine.

But going on a bicycle is *in bicicletta,* whilst arriving on a bicycle is *con bicicletta* - with a bicycle.

Going on foot is *a piede* whilst standing on your feet is *in piedi.*

Going to the sea is *al mare* but

Going to the mountains in *in montagne.*

As I write, these are the easy ones which we knew, but there are hundreds more which seem to have no logic about them at all. How could our poor deputy teacher expect to make us understand them, something we are still trying to do several years later?

Despite these last two weeks, we would have come again had the higher classes been able to give us what we wanted. We wanted conversational Italian which would let us talk to anyone we might meet in that country. Higher courses, we were told, dealt more with Italian literature or commerce but not just plain, ordinary talking. If we were going to go to school again, we would have to go somewhere else.

Chapter 6

Cesenatico

Our experience of the University for Foreigners at Perugia had made us determined to continue our studies in Italy, as well as at home. In England we had private classes every week from a charming Italian lady who had lived in this country for many years. She was also our instructor at an Adult Education Centre in the borough.

Trying to learn a foreign language in one's own country has its drawbacks. One can go to classes, read books, do exercises and buy foreign newspapers, but most of the time one is exposed to one's own language. In the country whose language one is trying to learn, one is constantly surrounded by it, and the longer one is there the better. We felt that in England, excellent though our classes were, we were doing little more than marking time. If we were to continue to improve we needed to find another school. But how? This is a question many have asked since. How did you find out where to go?

I first went to the Italian Tourist Agency in London. They were not able to help me, or not directly, anyway. They referred me to the Italian Cultural Institute in Belgrave Square, which was exceedingly helpful. I didn't even need to go there. A telephone call to ask if I could be supplied with a list of private language schools in Italy met with an immediate and favourable response.

'Of course. Please send us a large, stamped, self - addressed envelope and we will let you have all the information you need.'

It came quickly. There was information about perhaps twenty schools in various parts of Italy. It seemed unreasonable to write to them all so we began by crossing off those places we did not want to go to. We eliminated a couple more in big cities, feeling that we could integrate more easily in a small town.

I wrote to about six asking for details; prices of the courses, in either a formal class with other students, or for just the two of us, information about the availability of rented accommodation nearby, etc. Four replies were rather formal without answering all our questions, leaving two which sent us everything we asked for, including attractive brochures. One of these was in the mountains north of Perugia, which sounded very pleasant; the other was on the Adriatic coast at a town called Cesenatico.

Appealing though the mountains were, *in montagna* to use the right proposition, the idea of being by the sea was more attractive - *al mare*. This was not the only consideration. The letter we had received from Cesenatico was the most personal of all the responses. The director,

Professor Luigi Foshi, was undoubtedly attracted by the educational challenge such as two old folks like us were presenting to him. He offered to make any arrangements we liked. We settled for what he called 'semi individual' tuition, meaning for the two of us alone for the month of September 1992.

We asked him if he could find us a convenient apartment. He could, he replied, but we would be better living with an Italian family. Perhaps we would, we answered, but we felt we needed a degree of privacy, and we would like an apartment after all. It was all arranged, he replied again. We would have the best of both worlds in an apartment comprising part of a house, with the owners living in the other part. Moreover, he added, as a final inducement, there were twelve tortoises in the garden!

By this time he had dropped the formal Italian style of address for letters. I had been *Egregio Professore* - Eminent Professor - at the beginning, and I had addressed him similarly. Then it became *Caro Professore* - Dear Professor - and soon we were *Cari* Jack and Hazel and he was *Caro* Luigi. We were getting more and more excited about our projected visit and couldn't wait to go - *non vediamo l' ora* - or 'we do not see the hour', as it goes in Italian.

Cesenatico is on the Adriatic coast, south of Ravenna and north of Rimini. The province is Emiglia - Romagna and the coastal region is sometimes called the Italian Riviera. It is reached by driving east along the A14 from Bologna, where we had evolved a swift routine for getting away. As soon as we passed immigration Hazel went off to the Hertz desk while I waited for the luggage. By the time I came along the paperwork was done and we were ready to go. We were often away in little more than half an hour.

This time we had to ring Luigi from the airport to tell him of our arrival. It was Sunday afternoon and he wanted to be there to meet us when we reached Cesenatico. He gave us some rough directions which I tried to follow, but didn't take in completely. The school was bound to be well known, I thought, in such a small place. We should not have any trouble. It is true that Cesenatico is not large town, but we did not find the school at our first attempt. We found a police station, however, and I went in to ask for directions.

Could he please direct us to the Istituto Studium?

No, he had never heard of it.

But we had corresponded with the professor there, Professor Foschi.

He was instantly galvanised into activity.

'*Ah Foschi,*' he shouted. '*Si Foschi. Va Bene.*'

He produced a map of the town, showing us where we were and where we had to go.

This was an experience which would be repeated many times when the name of Professor

Foschi was mentioned. He was clearly a well - known person and each time his name came up some of his reflected glory rubbed off onto us.

We followed the instructions of the *poliziotto*, parked just around the corner from the *Istituto* and rang the bell. The door was opened by the man himself - a large man, indeed huge, and very jovial with it. He was wearing faded jeans and a faded denim jacket. I do not recall seeing him dressed in anything else throughout our stay. We were welcomed effusively, greeted, in fact, as if we were the old friends which we soon became. We settled one or two financial matters and he told us that our teacher was to be a lady from Rimini, called Giovanna. This would be our timetable - since we were only two people he was sure two hours of intense teaching Monday to Friday would be more than sufficient, and he was quite correct in this. Then, obviously showing that he felt there was more to life than study, he informed us that the best time for the beach was the morning, since it then had the sun, as the town faced East. We would be taught from two to four in the afternoon. In a country where we had been used to everything being closed between one o'clock and five this was a surprise. Presumably he knew the local climatic conditions and we had no objections. Now he would take us to our apartment.

The flat which had been arranged for us was little more than three hundred metres from the school at Number twenty, Via Donizetti. Our hosts were the Panzavolta family; Egidio and Sofia, the parents, Rocco, the elder son and Matteo the younger, and then a gap to Monica, who was eleven. They were a charming family and welcomed us warmly, showing us into the apartment.

It was on the ground floor of the house and they lived above, their home being reached by an outside staircase. We had a pleasant bedroom, a nicely tiled bathroom with shower - no reading in the bath this time - and a large kitchen with a settee along one wall. We were delighted to see thick, turkey towels in the bathroom; normally Italian towels are thin, tea-cloth type objects which dry poorly.

It seemed we had everything we needed except, at the moment, bread, butter and milk for breakfast. Sofia said she would be glad to let us have some or, if we preferred, we could go along to a little shop not far away, which, even on Sunday, would be open at five o'clock. Monica would show us the way. Moreover, here was a pot of plum jam we might enjoy! And, she added, we were of course expected for dinner that evening at 7:30.

Our luck, it seemed, was in and no mistake. We quickly unpacked and went outside to take in our surroundings. Via Donizetti was a narrow one-way street - that is to say it should have been, but it was not uncommon to see cars driving up it in the wrong direction. The houses were modern, and almost all had an outside staircase, suggesting that most were apartments for two or even three families. Each had a small garden in front for flowers and a bigger one at the back for vegetables. Egidio and Sofia grew vegetables of all kinds and they said we could help ourselves whenever we wished. Each house had a sliding metal gate letting cars in and out easily, including our rental car, which was tucked down the side of the house in a position from which we could drive out whenever we wished.

With our natural English reserve, we were somewhat apprehensive about dining with the family that night. Perhaps a gin and tonic might help us. I have been influenced all my life by a sentence I remember from the physiology book I used as a student - the only sentence I remember, in fact. 'Alcohol,' it read, 'relaxes the rigid self - control which inhibits the true enjoyment of congenial company.' We agreed.

Our natural self-control was soon relaxed, but more by the hospitality of our hosts than by the gin. We had a delightful meal of a creamy risotto, a chicken casserole and cheese, all accompanied by Egidio's home - made wine.

We learned about the family. Egidio was a taxi driver - *un autista* - Rocco had a job in a sports complex and Matteo was a civil servant. Monica, of course, was still at school. It was a very friendly gathering and we realised quickly that, although we would be formally at school for only two hours each day, our education in this family would go on all the time.

Our first morning was spent changing money at the bank around the corner, shopping at the nearby Co-op - pronounced 'coop' as in hencoop - and driving along the waterfront looking for the best place to visit the beach. Italians go in for highly organised beach activity, paying for a table and lounging chairs which are set out in long rows, presenting a spectacle of regimentation which had no appeal for us. We soon found a 'free beach' with very few people around. Our mornings were spent there, sometimes reading our Italian grammars sometimes not. Hazel bathed, but did not go further out than a statue of the Madonna which was placed on a pedestal some 150 metres from the water's edge. This being the Adriatic, the water's edge showed only a minimal tide movement at any time. We walked with our feet in the water and soaked up the sun which shone every day throughout our stay.

Luigi, as we were now calling him, was right that two hours of instruction each day would be sufficient for us. To have had more would have undoubtedly have been biting off more than we could chew - or in Italy, 'to take a step too long for the leg', or *far il passo piu lungo della gamba.* Our teacher, Giovanna, kept us going without respite and covered a great deal of ground. She was principally a teacher of Latin and Greek; she had no English. This occasionally made explanation a little difficult when we came to a word we did not understand. It is surprising though, how a synonym can be found or a picture drawn which soon conveys the meaning. Giovanna was a good teacher with only one drawback - she was a chain smoker!

At the end of the lesson, around four each day, we returned home for tea in the true English fashion. Boiling water to make tea in Italy is a surprisingly difficult task. None of the kitchens where we have lived has had a kettle, to say nothing of a teapot. Sofia obligingly produced a kettle but it was new and she had clearly gone out to buy it for us.

Outside our front door there was a table with four comfortable chairs where we took our tea whilst going over the day's lessons. In the mornings it was even more pleasant, and we sipped our coffee there in the gentle warmth of the morning sun, watching the local inhabitants going to work or to school. Whenever Egidio, and especially Sofia, saw us they would come across for a chat - *far quattro chiacchiere*, literally four chats. Sofia came in and out on her bicycle - *in bicicletta* - three or four times each day, almost always bringing home some shopping. Heavy shopping bags are not easy to carry on a bicycle, and she preferred to shop little and often at the Co-op.

Everyone seemed to cycle in Cesenatico but the confusing thing was they didn't at all mind which side of the road they travelled along. It was commonplace, when driving through the town, to find a bicycle coming towards us on our side; until we got used to it our immediate reaction always was that somehow, we had got onto the wrong side. We even went out a couple of times on bicycles ourselves but we always kept to the side roads; not for many years had either of us been on a bicycle and we decided that we were safer on foot - *a piedi*. Egidio was far from a mere cyclist of necessity. He was virtually a professional. Dressed up in his tight black shorts, yellow shirt and black and yellow cap on his racing bicycle he was a sight to see. Soon after we arrived he popped out one evening for a spin - thirty kilometres!

Before long we abandoned the Co-op for a more pleasant supermarket which we visited each day on our way back from the beach. We would pick up our simple lunch of bread, prosciutto or salami and cheese after having a chat with the manager. He naturally knew Luigi Foshi and when he asked us where we were living and we mentioned the Panzavolta family he cried at once, 'Ah Egidio. We were at school together.'

Cesenatico was that kind of place, where so many people knew each other. There was, for example, a small hut not far from our home where *piadine* were sold - a kind of flat bread on which one could pile anchovies, meats, or cheese. The lady who sold them was Luigi's aunt!

Cesenatico is a pretty seaside resort which caters to tourists, but only to a serious extent in July and August. In September it is idyllic. It's chief feature is a short canal designed in the year 1502 by no less a person than Leonardo da Vinci. There is no natural harbour, but fishing boats can come up the canal into the centre of the town; larger cruiser - type ships tie up nearer the canal mouth. The final stretch of the canal is now closed and a road crosses it. There is a maritime museum - *Il Museo della Mariniera* - in which beautifully reconstructed and painted fishing boats of long ago are preserved. When their brightly coloured sails are set they make a striking picture. We regretted that we have never been able to see them at Christmas time when the largest boat becomes a crib - *un presepio* - with life-sized figures beautifully dressed and illuminated, to judge by a Christmas card which Giovanna sent us.

It was to this harbour that we strolled, sometimes during the day but always in the evening. We had quickly fallen into a pleasant, gentle routine once our day's work was over. If we dined at one of the many simple restaurants along the quay we repaired afterwards to a cafe for a brandy - *un Vecchio Romagna*. If we dined at home we wandered out later for an ice-cream - *un gelato*. Hazel is addicted to Italian gelati, and

is an expert at assessing their quality. The gelati
of Cesenatico passed with flying colours, and
have since become the yardstick by which all
subsequent gelati in Italy are judged. Small,
medium or large sizes were available, but we
never got further than small, which we ate slowly
and thoughtfully, watching the world go by.

The harbour wall in Cesenatico is not to be
compared with the Corso Vanucci at Perugia,
but there is much to see. Families ride slowly by
on their bicycles and then ride slowly back again.
Young men with their girls and older men with
their wives stroll by. One small child, who could
not have been more than two, trotted up and
down, up and down, for hours until she was
collected by her mother and carried off to bed,
but never before ten o' clock. Perhaps the
strangest sight was to see a group of men sitting
in a cafe eating ice-cream and talking, always
talking.

We began to identify some of the locals and
they us. Each evening, as we strolled past the
Institute towards the harbour, we exchanged
greetings with an old couple - old even by our
standards - who sat on straight-backed chairs
outside their front door. The old lady had a
wonderfully lined face with crinkly crow's feet -
or in Italian - *zampa di gallina* - hen's feet around
her eyes. We always said *buona sera* on our way
to the harbour, and if they were there when we
returned we said *buona notte*, good night, a

salutation only uttered when you don't expect to see that person again until tomorrow.

With fresh fish coming right into the harbour every day, what else would we eat? Hazel believes that she did not eat meat for a month and even I, a carnivore if ever there was one, probably had meat only two or three times. Some fish were familiar, some not. We both enjoy mussels - *cozze* - which were always available as well as *vongole* - small clams - *sogliola* - sole - *triglia* - mullet and octopus and squid, of which my portion was always available for the cat. We dined out one evening with Luigi, who introduced us to a fish called *coda di rospo*. A rospo is a kind of toad, and we supposed that the fish, which may have been a type of monk fish, was extremely ugly; its tail however was delicious. The new experience we enjoyed most of all, however, was a small fish called *canocchia*, found only in Adriatic waters, but almost good enough to make a special journey to sample. Our Italian dictionary refers to it a *un piccolo crostaceo marino comestible* - a small sea crustacean which is eatable - but it is more than that, far more.

Our last evening was spent like our first, dining at home with the Panavoltas. We had a feast of wonderful fish, bought that morning straight off the boat. It was, if possible, a more convivial evening that our first one. Both Egidio and Sofia were insistent we should come back again next year, and we decided there and then that we would.

Luigi came down the following morning to see us off. We had finished our packing, but had to reopen two bags to fit in six bottles of home - made wine which Egidio insisted we take with us. Somehow we managed to fit them in, saying goodbye to our friends as they waved us off in our little car - until the Spring.

To arrive back in a place with pleasant memories and to find it just the same is a rare treat. We savoured our return as we turned off the main road into the town. But something was happening. Cars travelling along several streets were being temporarily held up by the police. There was evidently a cycle race. Would Egidio be in it? Perhaps he would win?

He didn't win, but he stayed the course - just - and what a course. The race was called the 'nine hills race' and my memory is that the contestants travelled a total of one hundred kilometres, give or take a kilometre, during the course of which they cycled up nine mountainous roads and down the other side. We were allowed to carry on to the Via Donizetta once the cyclists had passed by, and we were greeted effusively by Sofia. At that precise moment Egidio arrived but we were not greeted by him at all. He was speechless with exhaustion, gasping for breath, mutely holding our his hand for something to drink, water, wine, whatever, it did not matter. We left Sofia to resuscitate him and descended the stairway to await her outside the flat.

This time we were not in the same flat. There was great excitement in the household. Matteo was to be married to a girl called Monica from a nearby village: so very soon there would be two Monicas in the family. Sofia and Egidio had done everything possible to give the young couple a good start to their married life, which meant modernising and redecorating the apartment we had during the our last visit. We were given a conducted tour at once and we agreed that Matteo and Monica were a lucky pair; we could scarcely recognise the apartment we had known, so beautifully had it been transformed.

By contrast, at least this was our first thought, we were to be in the garage next door. It wasn't like that at all, of course. The young people's flat was indeed adjacent to what had been a garage, but one into which Egidio seldom put his car. Now it had been converted into another apartment which was, in almost every respect, like the one we had occupied in September. We felt at home at once.

We were invited to the wedding, which presented me with a sartorial problem. I had not come with my Sunday best - *con gli abiti migliori* - indeed I had neither jacket nor tie. I had gradually brought to Italy fewer and fewer formal clothes, as I realised how informal most Italian attire was. A quick perusal of my wardrobe, if that is not too strong a word, left us wondering if a faded batik shirt I had bought ten years earlier in Singapore might just do. Sofia said not to worry - *non importa* - so we settled for that. I was eventually able to compare my attire with that of the other male guests and I was not too out of place.

There was one sad fly in the ointment. Monica's father disapproved of the match and was very angry *molto arrabiato* and would not be attending the wedding. We had little to do with the preparations, and our sessions with Giovanna began as before from two to four, every afternoon. This time, however, we had stipulated to Luigi that we did not want *la grammatica*, only *la conversazione*. We talked about all kinds of subjects during these periods - what was in the newspapers, what the Italian politicians were doing, which seemed to be no secret, what life was like in England and how it was different from life in Italy. Since Giovanna was a Greek scholar, we talked about Greek mythology and we were surprised to learn that Pandora did not keep all the evils of the world in a box, but in a vase - *il vaso do Pandora*. These conversation sessions were, if anything, more exhausting than the previous *grammatica* ones but no less enjoyable.

On the day, before the wedding, the house was decorated with flowers, bunting and bouquets; even our rent-a-car had white rosettes tied to it. Could we do anything to help, we asked Sofia. She replied that we could go off in our car and collect the confetti. We set off, following her instructions and were surprised to find that we were outside a sweet shop. We were even more surprised when, having asked for the confetti, we were given three boxes of sugared almonds. We did not know that confetti means something quite different in the Italian language. Confetti are eaten and rice is thrown at weddings.

The *matrimonio* was to be held in a small church in Monica's village. The stream of wedding cars approaching the church was met by the delightful Italian custom of a barrage of horns from all the cars travelling in the opposite direction. Several wedding customs in Italy differ from our own. The Sunday wedding is one. Another difference is that the guests wait outside until the bride and groom arrive, then the bride goes in on the arm of her father and groom with his mother, all the guests following. Since Monica's father was not to be there the young couple were to go in together. We were pleased to see Matteo approach the car as soon as Monica arrived and hand her a bouquet.

The reception in a hotel by the beach was a lavish party and Hazel and I had been considerably misled about the extent of the hospitality being offered. A very long table groaned with canapes, sandwiches, prosciutto, salami, pastry dishes, rolls and butter and other things we couldn't identify. This was a marvellous spread, we said to each other as we helped ourselves - modestly of course. It was just as well since this was merely the antipasta. It was followed by spaghetti and *dolces* of various kinds. Bottles of wine, in unfailing supplies, raised the already elevated spirits of the wedding party even higher, and we learned what the 'confetti' were for.

Two of the bridegroom's friends carried around a large basket of rosettes made from the sugared almonds that we had bought from the sweet shop. Two more friends carried around a second basket. The idea was that each guest took a rosette and made a contribution into the second basket to give the young couple a sound financial send-off. There were no formal speeches, but there was some boisterous horseplay from Matteo's friends, and no doubt from Monica's too, but we were unable to distinguish which guest belonged to whom. Several songs were sung, which may have been of questionable nature, judging by the laughter from the crowd; we were quite unable to understand the words.

Work the next day was an anticlimax. Our routine this time was just as it had been before. We visited the beach in the mornings. Hazel bathed and I paddled, and we walked long distances with our feet in the water. We watched some man catching small crabs and others playing *boccia* in a somewhat makeshift *bocciadromo*. We paid close attention to the game and the shouted conversation of the players, but like Omar Kyhyam, we came out by the same door as in we went - no wiser.

Luigi, all the time, was keeping a friendly eye on our progress and on our leisure activities. He had previously taken us northwards to visit a lovely cathedral called Pomposo, taking us afterwards to nearby Porto Romano to eat eels - *anguille* - fresh from the sea. This time he took us to Ravenna.

There are four incomparable places to visit in Ravenna - Sant' Apollinaris in Classe, Sant' Apollinaris Nuovo, the Basilica di San Vitale and the Battistero Neoniano. The mosaics in these building have a beauty beyond belief. Perhaps the spacious elegance of Sant' Apollinaris in Classe appealed most, but when one is surrounded by such an abundance of majestic mosaics, comparison is futile; all were marvellous beyond imagining.

Before we left on this second occasion we had a celebration dinner at a restaurant called *Il Ristornate dell Aia*. An *aia* is a threshing floor, and the restaurant was in a gigantic barn-like building a short distance outside the town. We drove down a long rutted lane which seemed to go nowhere, but suddenly we were confronted by a huge car park, virtually full of the cars of the diners who had got there before us.

The place was crowded. There was no such thing as reserving a table, and we waited with varying degrees of impatience. Eventually we were led into a vast hall crowded with people eating, drinking, shouting, gesticulating, and at one table, singing. Luigi made the choice and we were served with large grills of meat, which seemed to be the only thing available, a big bowl of raw vegetables, which was plonked in the middle of the table along with jugs of red and white wine. It was a fun evening with guffaws of laughter and lots of banter between our friends, and our own tongues were loosened with more rapid, but no doubt less accurate Italian which seemed, nevertheless, to be understood. Hazel, dreaming of the sea-fresh fish of Cesenatico, might have enjoyed it less than I, carnivore that I am.

We realised, by now, that we were approaching the end of our last visit to Cesanatico. The friends we had made were quite delightful and the town was charming, but we like to seek our new places. Also, that part of Emiglia Romagna had, for us, one drawback - we did not find our week-end jaunts into the surrounding countryside as enjoyable as others we had spent elsewhere. If we were to go to school again it would have to be somewhere else. Our goodbyes this time were final ones. There would be telephone calls and Christmas cards in the future but no more visits - not even for the *canocchie.*

Chapter 7

Urbania

There was no immediate prospect of our return to Italy. In September, 1993, we had to go to Australia and in April, 1993, to the U.S.A.. By the time we returned from America we had not been to Italy for a year and we were both suffering withdrawal symptoms. We needed to go back to school.

The Italian Cultural institute provided us with another list which contained the names of a few schools we did not remember seeing before. Two of these seemed especially attractive. One was on the Tuscany coast and the other in a town called Urbania, in the province of Le Marche.

We finally decided on the latter for several reasons. The stated object of the school was not only to teach the Italian language but to include instruction in various aspects of Italian culture. Students were encouraged to integrate with the townsfolk; classes would be small, ten or so at the most, and they included every grade from rank beginners to the most advanced - in which group we were not. A small test, taken on the day of arrival, would allow one to be put into the correct class. In addition the school would arrange whatever accommodation the student required - an apartment of whatever size, or accommodation with a family, or a room in a hotel or in a hostel. It all sounded very well organised - and so it proved. We signed on for a three week course in September 1994, and the school arranged an apartment, provided the name of our landlady, and gave us the address and telephone number.

Urbania is reached by driving along the A14 out of Bologna towards the Adriatic coast, then past the Cesenatico turn off to the outskirts of the town of Pesaro, then inland for perhaps 40 kilometres. Our journey got off to a most encouraging start.

I had driven for perhaps twenty kilometres out of Bologna when we pulled into a lay - bye to change drivers. There was already a car parked there and as soon as we stopped, a couple got out to ask us the way to Pavlova! Few things are quite so satisfactory, when one is in a foreign country, as to give directions to nationals. We produced our large scale map and showed them that they had missed a big road junction just outside Bologna; they would need to go back again to this point. They still seemed confused about how to do this until we pointed out that there was an exit road just ahead, and all they needed to do was get off there, go ever the bridge and join the other carriageway going back towards Bologna. They smiled and thanked us and we beamed with pride - *orgoglio* - and continued on our way feeling very superior.

We reached Urbania easily, since we were travelling in the early afternoon, during the hours of the *siesta* and we stopped at the entrance to the town to ask directions to the Via Molino dei Signori. We received detailed instructions; it was no use trying to go through the narrow streets of the town, our informant told us, we should continue on around the ring road, turn right across the bridge and then left into the road we wanted. We were to keep a look out for *il ponte*, he stressed, and then he proudly said it in English 'bridge,' beaming all over his face as he did so.

Number twenty, Via Molino dei Signori was a modern house whose owner, as it happened, was away for a few days. This produced no problem. A neighbour appeared like magic. She had been detailed off to let us in and show us around. A few other neighbours gathered to give us encouragement. Where could we leave the car, we asked; outside the house, half on the pavement, like everybody else, they said. We could see along the road that this was indeed true, and we still think of Urbania as the town where the cars occupied the pavements and the pedestrians walked in the road.

Our apartment was on the second floor and was quite ample for our needs; there was a hall, bedroom, bathroom with a shower - no reading in the bath again - a large kitchen and a patio where we could sit outside if we wished and enjoy a marvellous view over the Urbanian countryside.

We opened drawers and cupboards, as one does, to find out what was available for our needs. We found numerous large saucepans, five frying pans but, of course, no kettle. It was now 4 o'clock and we had to decide which container would be most suitable for boiling water for tea. We finally settled on the deepest of the five frying pans and brewed up. We had brought tea with us and had written ahead to ask Polda, our landlady, to buy bread, milk and butter for us. We enjoyed a leisurely cup of tea on our patio and then decided we should stroll into the town and find out where the school was and where we could dine that evening.

The neighbour who had let us in had told us which way to go and had said it was only a walk of five to ten minutes. Despite this we exchanged *buona sera* with several more ladies before we reached the end of the Via dei Signori; integration with the locals did not look as if it was going to be a problem. We passed the Cafe Foschi - did Luigi's influence really extend this far? - crossed an elegant bridge and there was our school, a large stone building in a narrow street, immediately opposite a church with the interesting name of *La Chiesa dei Morti* - The Church of the Dead. We later went in to see a display of same twenty mummies which had been discovered behind the altar during renovations a century or so ago. One of them still showed unmistakable sign of having been a Down's Syndrome child.

The school was closed so we continued on for a short distance, past two more churches and into one of the main streets of the town. The information centre was just opening and we went in to ask about restaurants. The young man within obligingly produced a map and, despite the fact that he turned it to face us, and it was upside down for him, quickly made four of five crosses on it to show us where we could dine. 'Were they far away?' we asked. 'Nothing is far away in Urbania,' he answered, and there was one about 50 metres down the road. And to make us feel at home perhaps, he added, 'It is called Big Ben.'

We were to dine at Big Ben that evening and on several more occasions during our stay. The food was always excellent and the other diners made an interesting study. One solitary old man seemed always to have a table in the corner. Groups of varying size came, often with children and even babies. One lady brought along eight children one evening and, having got them all seated, left them to their own devices. An American couple with no Italian appeared on one occasion, whilst several of our fellow students became, like ourselves, regular diners.

We established a good relationship with the *capo* who was a mine of information about local wine. We invariably left the choice to him and we were never disappointed. Only on one occasion did I venture a small comment when he had produced a bottle of red wine which seemed as though it might be a little cool. Not concerned simply to reassure us, he opened a cupboard and produced a special thermometer which he introduced into the neck of the bottle, and in a few moments said, *Va bene. Diciotto gradi* - eighteen degrees.

As we walked across the bridge towards our school the following morning we had no notion of the treat that was in store for us. Perugia had been fine, Cesenatico, with the charming friends we had made, was splendid, but this school was just superb.

We passed through the large double doors into the customary stone - flagged hall. Three black students, seeing our uncertainty, directed us up to the second floor to the secretary's office. We were later to learn that they were seminarians from Nigeria, and they were the first of a number of religious students we met during our stay.

As we took the first step up the stairs I wondered how old this building was since generations, or even centuries, of feet had worn an indentation in the first step into which one could probably have poured a bottle of wine.

The secretary to the Director welcomed us and ticked us off on her list. We discussed certain financial matters, such as how much we still had to pay in addition to the deposit we had sent some months before. We were surprised to find that we were expected to pay in cash - *in contanti* - the reason being, perhaps, that with students coming from all over the world, some of their cheques might be very difficult to process; far easier to let the bank do it first. We were given a test, which we were not expected to do then, but to take it home that afternoon, bringing it back the next morning. Meanwhile, we would be put into a temporary class and, to determine which, we were asked what we had already done at other schools.

Il congiuntivo? - the present subjective - *Si.*

Il congiuntivo imperfetto? - past subjective - *Si.*

Il passato remoto? - *Si.*

Le preposizioni? - prepositions - *piu o meno* - more or less.

That seemed to satisfy the secretary, who gave each of us a free textbook which we would be following and a free note book to write in. We were asked not to write in the text book yet, in case our class had to be changed. We were taken along to *Aula Dante* and introduced to our teacher, Andrea.

With one exception we had been fortunate with our teachers so far and with Andrea we were particularly lucky. He had a delightful personality, a clear method of teaching and he changed the subject we were studying several times each lesson, so that we never got bored. He was already on familiar terms with the class who had been with him for a week, and he asked us at once of he could use *il tu*. There are two modes of address in Italian, as in French - the polite, used between people who did not know each other well, when 'you' is *lei*, and the informal used between friends and with children, when 'you' is *tu*. We were only too pleased to be informal and give each other *il tu*.

With our arrival the class became ten in number. There was Stefano, a South Korean divinity student who was hoping to learn enough Italian to go to Rome to study theology.

Gunnar, an Austrian boy who formed part of the school's team in a sports competition which was held later.

Daniela, an Austrian girl who seemed to have the best Italian amongst us - and excellent English too.

Eva, a somewhat serious German girl.

Ulrica, an outgoing German who translated children's books into her own language, and was no doubt hoping to do so from Italian.

Beneditta, a Danish singer, trying to improve her knowledge and pronunciation for her profession.

Alban, an American monk, also hoping to go to Rome to study, and a Japanese lady whose name we never learned, but who spoke very precise Italian.

We accomplished our first morning satisfactorily we felt, although it was hard going at times - *motlo intenso*. We believed that we had been able to keep up with the class and we hoped that we would not have to move. Now we must go to the bank and draw out sufficient cash to pay our bills. I do not normally walk around with more than four hundred pounds in cash on my person but, strangely, had no anxiety about doing so in Urbania - but I went back to the secretariat as soon as I could to pay.

Lunchon on our balcony that day was particularly welcome. We had been charmed by our teacher, pleased with our fellow students, and delighted to have kept our end up. All we needed to do now was to make a satisfactory showing in our test to make sure we stayed with Andrea. We tackled the tests in the afternoon and handed them in the following morning; they contained, Andrea said to our delight, *pochi errori* - few errors - and we could stay with the class.

At the same time as we were given our test we had also received the programme for the week's work, and it was clear that no opportunity to instruct the students in language and culture had been missed. We should have no problem filling our days. This was what was in store.

Mornings

Every morning, Monday to Friday, there was three hours of language teaching - 9 am to 12.30 pm with a break - *una pausa* - from 10.50 to 11.20 for shopping. Many shops closed around 12.30 and food for lunch had to be bought before school started in the morning or around 11 am.

On Saturday mornings, provided the class wished it, two hours of tuition would be provided. Andrea even came in to give us a class one Saturday morning, despite the fact that he was going to a wedding at 1 pm.

Afternoons and Evenings

Monday afternoon was free but there was a cultural evening at 9 pm - a film perhaps or a musical evening.

Tuesday was a busy day. From 2.30 to 4.30 pm there was a choice of Italian literature, Italian political and social life or Italian conversation. From 4.30 to 5.30 pm there was a lecture on Italian art from a charming lady called Donatella. We should later learn that she had another string to her bow or, as Italians say, *il piede in due scarpe* - the foot in two shoes. From 6.40 onwards, until goodness knows when, we had the class of the week - Italian Cookery.

Wednesday afternoons had no classes but there was always an outing arranged to Urbino or to other nearby towns. Buses were provided for a modest charge.

Thursday was as Tuesday but without, sadly, the art lecture. Friday was as Monday.

Saturday afternoon was, in theory, free, but on one Saturday Donatella took anyone who wished around the art treasures of Urbania, whilst on another there was a match - games and competitions of all kinds - between the young people of Urbania and those of Urbino with a team from the school taking part.

On Sundays there was an all day excursion to Assisi or Florence of some caves not too far away with stalactites and stalagmites - *le stalatitte e le stalagmitte*. A busy week to be sure.

We went on one of these Wednesday excursions to the famous city of Urbino, one of the finest achievements of the Italian Renaissance. Under Duke Frederico da Montefeltro, who ruled it from 1444 to 1482, it became a city renowned for the beauty of its buildings, the magnificent artistic and literary collections of its Palazzo Ducale and its enlightened administration. Here in the Ducal Palace we were able to renew our acquaintance with the artist Piero della Francesca. We saw what is probably his most bizarre picture called *La Flagellazione* - the Scourging. What Piero had in mind in this work had been the subject of much debate, but it seems to me to be a study in supreme indifference to suffering.

Three men dressed in 15th century costumes hold a discussion in the foreground, oblivious of the torment of Christ who is being scourged behind them. The same artist has another Madonna and Child - the Madonna di Senigallia - recognisably the same lady as we had seen in the Madonna del Parto, in Monterchi and the Misericordia Polyptych in Sansepolcro. There is a strange *Citta Ideale* - ideal city - which, although showing Piero's mastery of perspective, is without people and has the appearance of a ghost town.

It was in Urbino, in a house half way up a steep hill, that Raffaello Sanzio , whom we refer to as Rapheal, was born in 1483. Like the birthplace of Piero della Francesca in Sansepolcro, this house has also become a museum and contains many works by the artist and others. It is now the centre of L'Accademia Raffaello. We were able to see two of Raffaello's finest pictures in the Ducal Palace; one is a study of St. Catherine of Alexandria, who stands on her monstrous spiked wheel, the Catherine wheel of bonfire night, holding the palm of martyrdom in her hand; the other is called 'A Portrait of a Lady' but is usually known as '*La Muta*' - the mute one, perhaps because she stares so mutely and serenely from the canvas at the thousands upon thousands who have stared back at her over the centuries.

There was much more to do but we could no longer absorb it. Refreshment called and Urbino is full of little cafes where it can be obtained. We joined a large man whom we recognised as coming from our school and discussed the sights of Urbino with him in Italian only for him to tell us later that he was a priest from Dallas, Texas. He was wearing a snappy line in sports wear too - but then there is an old Italian proverb which states *L'abito non fa il monaco* - the habit doesn't make a monk!

We had already visited other centres to which excursions were made but having our own car we could go where we liked. We explored some of the smaller towns of Le Marche, several with melodious names - *St Angelo in Vado, Mercatello sul Metauro, Borgopace* - peaceful village - and Sassoferraro. We travelled through *La Gola del Furlo* - literally 'The Throat of the Gallery,' which was a spectacular narrow passage between towering cliffs: here, we were told, a Roman consul had built a road to unite Rome to the north of Italy and, towards its end, Roman soldiers had excavated a tunnel - in Latin, *Forulum*, hence Furlo. We stopped in another village to watch a bride and groom being photographed after their Sunday wedding - and we directed a late guest who was lost and who asked us the way. We got lost ourselves, but with all the time in the world, what did it matter? We were sure to find our way back eventually. We found a pleasant place for our lunch *al sacco* - a picnic - and read our books in the car afterwards.

We visited a cemetery since Italian cemeteries have a fascination for Hazel. This one was most elaborate, with many family tombs where photographs of the dear departed were displayed and where flowers were regularly changed; it was all very neat and tidy and cared for by the many relatives whom we saw arriving, often with their children, during the time we were there. We lazed our weekends away, just as we had done at the start of it all in Tuoro sul Trasimeno, so as to be refreshed for Monday morning and whatever the next week's classes would bring.

Our days soon settled into a simple routine. Shopping for lunch - cheese, prosciutto, salami and beer - either before school started or during our *pausa*. If time permitted we joined the others for a cappuccino at a small nearby cafe. More serious shopping was done at a supermarket close to our apartment.

In the evenings we usually dined out. It was on one of these evenings that we discovered Donatella's 'foot in two shoes.' Having been to Big Ben a couple of times, we decided to try another restaurant, highly recommended by the man in the Information Centre, called Osteria del Cucco. An *osteria* is a kind of tavern and a *cucco* can mean a pet or a favourite thing, although it is more likely that it is a dialect form of *cuoco* - a cook. At any event, off we went to find this minute restaurant which could just squeeze in about fourteen diners - the cook was Donatella!

She was as skilful at cooking as she was at lecturing on art. Not the least interesting thing about the Cucco was its informality. Nothing was ever written down. Donatella always came out to tell her customers what dishes she was making that evening, describing her various pastas, each a mouth watering delicacy. Of course there was an antipasta before and a meat course after, if one wished, but one pasta dish, such as she cooked, was always sufficient for us. Our choice of wine was simple - red or white - and that having been decided and the meal consumed, a waitress consulted Donatella in the kitchen and came back to tell you that the price was Lire 26,000 or whatever - never expensive. The restaurant was generally full, and because it was so small, sharing a table was commonplace. One evening we shared a table with three Japanese who talked to each other all evening in Italian.

We rarely ate at home but one evening we did, strolling out afterwards to sample the *gelati* of Urbana. Mine was fine, but Hazel, judging hers by the standards of Cesenatico, only gave it eight out of ten.

All of our sessions, formal and informal, at the school were excellent but the high spot, beyond any doubt, was the class on *La Cucina Italiana* - Italian Cookery.

I had not gone to the first of these, thinking that the members of the class might have to do some of the cooking themselves; I am no great shakes as a cook, an interested spectator yes, but not a practitioner. Hazel went off with a group of others around 6.45 and I spent a dull evening at home, reading my paper back, eating a cold meal of prosciutto and feeling sorry for myself. My gloom was not lifted by finding that the flat had no corkscrew - *un cavatappi* - and I couldn't open the bottle of wine I had bought for sustenance. I contemplated breaking off the neck but thought better of it and settled for beer.

By 10.30 pm Hazel had not returned, nor had she by 11. I began to get worried but could think of nothing I could do. Finally at 11.30 pm I heard her key in the door and she came in beaming all over her face having had a marvellous time. To put it quite simply, the teacher had demonstrated the cooking of four dishes and the students had eaten them! I must certainly join that; no more lonely evenings when a party like that was on offer.

The following day I paid my fees for the remaining five lessons which worked out at the equivalent of thirty five pounds. That evening we drove off in our little car, giving a lift to a jovial Englishman called Stephen, an Engineer who was filling in time between jobs in Nepal. We drove for some six or seven kilometres then turned into a cart track which went up and up until we reached an old farm house behind which was the cook house, an immense barn which had been adapted, up to a point, for our cookery demonstrations.

I was introduced to our teacher, Francesca, a slight, dark lady with a flashing smile and a vivacious manner. She cooked magnificently but ate little, accounting not doubt for her slender build, which was further maintained by the distance she was obliged to cover to coordinate all her culinary activities. Her kitchen, if we can call it that, was scarcely trouble free. By the door, in the middle of one wall, were a fridge and an electric mixer. In the far right corner was a wood -burning oven, towards the left corner was a gas cooker, beyond which was a cold water sink. She demonstrated at a nearby wooden table and there was a long dining table in the left corner large enough to seat twelve or fourteen people.

We were not a large group. Apart from ourselves there were three Germans, an Austrian girl, two English boys, Paul and James, who were students of Italian at London University, Stephen and an Australian named Grant. Grant apparently had sold his house in Australia and was touring Europe with his wife Maxine and his three year old child. Because of babysitting requirements, both could not attend the classes, choosing instead to alternate evenings.

The demonstrations were wonderful to watch, especially when Francesca made ravioli.

She rolled out the pasta with a rolling pin that was at least a metre in length, perhaps more. To watch her roll and turn, roll and turn, was fascinating. From time to time she rolled the pasta completely onto the rolling pin and literally threw it along the length of the table, letting it unwind as it went. When the required thinness had been achieved, she piped small heaps of spinach mixture at short intervals along the whole length of half the pasta, leaving the other half alone. She then painted this half with egg white and folded it over the part containing the spinach portions. She ran the side of her hand along between the rows of spinach, vertically and horizontally and did the same with a pastry cutter to divide each into individual ravioli. The egg white, she said, would bind the pasta and none would open during the cooking - nor did it.

This was just one of her marvellous demonstrations which had her class spellbound. Since, as she was well aware, the understanding of Italian in the group was variable - Grant and his wife had little, for example - Francesca showed us each item she was using so that, if the word for it was not understood, the object itself would be recognised. Grant sat next to Hazel, who translated the difficult bit for him. After the demonstration was over we ate almost everything. The leftovers, Grant took home to his wife.

For each class everybody had to contribute five pounds towards ingredients. With that and the registration, wine included, every one of these gourmet meals cost only twelve pounds per person.

The conventional view that Italians eat only spaghetti and its variants was quickly demolished by Francesca.

On the first Tuesday, whilst I was having my solitary cold meal, and had demonstrated how pasta should be made in the manner just described for the ravioli. To accompany this she prepared two sauces, one of meat and the other of vegetables, since one member of the class was a vegetarian. There then followed *coniglio in porchetta* - a whole rabbit roasted with prosciutto and bacon. The meal ended with a superb *dolce*, a delicious sweet with walnuts. No wonder I was determined to join the class.

My introduction to Francesca's wonderful cooking was the finest lasagna I have ever had the pleasure to taste. She then prepared *saltimbocca alla romana* - very thin slices of veal to which a small piece of prosciutto and a sprig of sage had been attached by a tiny wooden stick and the whole thing cooked in the frying pan. Salt and pepper were applied only to the side without the prosciutto. *Zuppa inglese* - English soup, or trifle as cooked in Italy, finished this splendid repast. Generally *zuppa inglese*, whether in Italy or England, does little for either Hazel or me but Francesca's would have been taken any prize offered.

Our second week began with a risotto, beautifully prepared with small pieces of *salsicce* - spiced sausage. *Vitello con fungi* followed - veal with fresh mushrooms to which were added dried *porcini* mushrooms (a very special Italian delicacy which had been soaked for five hours.) Two *dolci* were then presented to us that evening; a *tiramisu* - Italy's finest sweet consisting of eggs, marscapone cheese, icing sugar, sponge fingers, a small amount of strong black coffee, Tia Maria (Hazel uses this but Francesca used brandy) and cocoa sprinkled on the top to finish. Our other *dolce* was *panna cotta* - literally cooked cream - exquisite.

By this time thoughts of what the next cookery class might bring was making it harder to concentrate on our lesson and a great deal of self disciple needed to be exerted to listen attentively to what Andrea was telling us. What we might be offered on Thursday continued to obtrude

Thursday brought the ravioli with pesto sauce about which I have already enthused. Included in this meal was a *teglia di verdura* - a dish of various vegetables cooked in a frying pan - and finally a *ciambellone* - a sweet cake made from eggs, sugar, lemon, milk and flour.

The Tuesday of our last week produced the only dish we did not enjoy; *pollo a pepperoni*. It was beautifully cooked but not worth cooking. Italians have a different method of preparing a chicken which consists, quite simply, of cutting it up into little pieces so that one gets a lot of bone and little flesh. We both gave up after struggling for a time and we concentrated on the *spaghetti alla carbonara* which followed and the *dolce di mela* - apple cake - after that.

Francesca was clearly determined to make our last evening something very special, as if all the others had not been! She prepared a huge dish of *minestrone* which was served with slices of bread warmed in the oven. We had a vegetable dish which she called *pepperonata,* a *focaccia* - a sort of bread like preparation with rosemary - and *pastella* - zuccini fried in batter. The main dish was *fegato alla veneziana* - succulent slices of liver lightly fried with wine, onions and parsley. Our never to be forgotten classes in Italian cookery ended with *castagnole* - small deep fried souffles, served with a raspberry sauce.

This wonderful evening became a family affair when we had a short visit from Francesca's two children, a boy of six and a girl of nine years of age. After that we gave Francesca a little present which she richly deserved. Addresses were exchanged and Francesca and Hazel promised to write to each other. They did; Francesca to say kindly how much she had enjoyed teaching us and Hazel to send her a recipe for Yorkshire pudding.

Andrea's classes seemed to go from strength to strength as Francesca's did. We covered so much ground a day, with homework to do as well, that we felt we were progressing as never before. We dealt with various aspects of Italian grammar and we did exercises and read articles from newspapers and magazines, which we then discussed.

One was an infinitely sad tale of a confidence man who had taken a large sum of money from a number of ignorant Sicilian families - all the money they had in some cases - to transport them, he said, to America. Taking advantage of their naivety and trust, he merely moved them along the coast and off - loaded them in another part of the island, making them believe that it was the land of plenty they had dreamed of.

Another concerned a radio ham who had made contact with a man living on a mysterious island in the middle of the Atlantic. The story stopped and we had to try to write how it might have ended. A third was a marvelously funny account of a man who had lost his driving licence and had to cope with all manner of Italian bureaucracy before he got another.

The Mafia, of course, was ubiquitous. Somewhat against our inclinations we learned several things about the organisation we had not known before. The subject seemed to hold a reluctant fascination for Andrea, who told us that Italy would be the richest nation in Europe, were it not for the Mafia. We had always thought of it under its common name, the Mafia, but evidently in Campania it was known as the *Cammorra*, and in Calabria as the *Drangheta*. The Italiano - American organisation was called the *Cosa Nostra* - our thing, a term which later became more generally used. It's distorted code of honour, where allegiance is shown only to itself, is referred to as *Onorata Societa* - honoured society; honour here signifying no more than total allegiance to the *Capo* or boss and the code of *Omerta* - *il Muro dell Omerta* - the wall of silence.

Different families may have their own *capo* but the *Capo di tutti capi* - the head of all heads - is the boss who is sometimes blasphemously referred to as the *Padrina* - the godfather.

The name which seemed to us to be the most suitable for the entire organisation was *La Piovra* - the octopus, or the bloodsucker or the vampire.

By common consent we left the Mafia to its own devices and returned to *la superstizione* and black cats, which we discussed long ago, it now seemed, in Perugia.

So by one means or another we were learning many aspects of the language of Italy, but not only about its language.

The expressed intention of the school had been that, in addition to learning the beautiful Italian language and culture, we should integrate into the life of the community. We achieved this with ease. Urbania is an ancient town but a small one. It had once been called Castel Durante but its name had been changed centuries earlier after a visit there by Pope Urban VIII. We had the impression that this change was not wholeheartedly accepted by its town folk, since almost every time the name Urbania was written, it was qualified by words such as 'Urbania, the ancient Castel Durante' or 'Urbania, once Castel Durante'. I don't suppose that they will ever change it back but I got the impression some would like to.

The *centro storico* of the town is full of character, narrow streets, arcaded sidewalks, tiny piazzas, food shops by the score, cafes, bars and restaurants, the latter ignored by us apart from Big Ben and the Osteria del Cucco. Italian cafe society is a strange chauvinistic one. With few exceptions only men are to be seen there; the women stay at home to do the work and the men, left at loose ends, stand around in groups in the piazzas or gravitate to the cafes and bars. We must, for example, have passed the Cafe Foschi four or five times every day, but only twice did we see a woman there. For the rest of the time it was full of men, talking, playing cards, talking, watching football on TV and talking.

Outside the *centro storico* there was modern Urbania but there was little of it and one was out in the country very quickly. We were able to stroll across a playing field from our apartment and down a long lane leading to an equestrian centre. It was while we were crossing this playing field one Saturday afternoon that we met *un filosofo* - a philosopher. He was working on his allotment - *lotto di terra* - and we walked over to see what he was growing. He stopped work and came across to talk to us. We admired his vegetables and eventually admitted, somewhat sheepishly, that we were students, but a lot older than usual.

Non importa. Tutta la vita è un esame, he answered - never mind, all of life is an examination. How true.

He told us the story about an English airman who had been sheltered in Urbania by an Italian family during the war and had eventually managed to escape. After the war he returned to find the family who had saved him. They had left, however, and the house in which they had lived was empty. He bought it and has lived there ever since, teaching English to anyone who is interested.

It was casual encounters such as this with another culture that we so much enjoyed during all our Italian trips. Soon this one would be over. One or two people had already gone - Paul and James back to the University of London, Stephen to take up another post, and Ulrica, who went to Florence to sit a national examination for her

Intermediate Italian Certificate. Before long our community would all be gone, scattered to the four winds, individuals once more with nothing in common except memories.

To our surprise the school had a grand send off waiting for us. At 11.30 am on our last day we all assembled in the meeting hall of the school for a final ceremony. There was an air of excitement everywhere. Cameras flashed, there were hugs and kisses and cheerful cries and high spirits. The teachers arrived, all ladies, apart from Andrea and one other man. Huge bouquets of flowers were produced by the grateful students for their instructors. In the middle of the table at the front with his secretary, holding two large boxes, was the director, Professor Pasotto.

He made a charming speech saying how good we all had been, how much he hoped that we had absorbed the ambience of Italy and its culture and how he hoped we would come again - some of us at any rate. To clamorous applause he then presented each student a large envelope containing a certificate of attendance, a group photograph which had been taken earlier in the grounds of the Ducal Palace, a placard with the face of Dante Alighiere on it - who was no beauty believe me - and several copies of the school prospectus which he hoped we would distribute amongst those of our friends who might be persuaded to come to Urbania.

It was a splendid final ceremony but, like all farewells a sad one. We have our certificates and we have our photographs to remember it by. I don't suppose that we will go again, but who knows - we might.

Other books from Summersdale